The Progressive Knitter

With patterns and illustrations throughout by the author and photography by Dudley Moss.

The Progressive Knitter

Maggie Whiting

B. T. BATSFORD LTD, LONDON

DEDICATION
To my mother, Joyce Runnicles, for first instilling in me a love of knitting, and to Keith for always being there.

ISBN 0 7134 5835 6

Typeset by Tameside Filmsetting Limited
Ashton-under-Lyne, Lancashire
and printed in Great Britain by
Anchor Brendon, Tiptree, Essex
for the publishers
B. T. Batsford Ltd
4 Fitzhardinge Street
London W1H 0AH

Contents

Acknowledgements

Many thanks to everyone who helped and encouraged me, especially the following people: Dudley Moss for his care and skill with the photography; Angela Peirce for her enthusiasm, time and effort helping me knit up the garments; Raymond Palmer for additional photographs; Natasha Mackenzie, Cyndi Holdsworth, Joanne Ratcliffe and Nick Whiting for modelling the garments; Anita Schuetz for checking the patterns; Doreen Lilley for typing the manuscript; Jan Messent for first bringing my name to the attention of Batsford; all my students who kindly lent me their work for publication; and Louise Simpson and Rachel Wright for their editorial help. Lastly, special thanks to my family for their forbearance while the book was in progress.

Location photography at Windlesham Arboretum, courtesy of Major Spowers. Yarn substitution symbols courtesy of Vogue Knitting. Excerpts from Chapter 19 first appeared in *Fashion & Craft* magazine, summer 1987. Knitting yarn symbol by Jane Rose (Batsford).

Introduction

My main purpose in writing this book is to inspire you to try out your own knitting ideas instead of following patterns blindly, without ever attempting to adapt or improve upon what you see. Many knitters long to be creative but lack the confidence to try because they have no idea where to begin. Haven't you ever wished you could alter styles to suit your own needs precisely? Maybe you have already managed to adapt a neckline or alter the shape of a sleeve. So why stop there? Why not carry on and learn how to design for yourself from the very beginning?

There is no mystique attached to designing as so many people think. Anyone can do it. In fact, it is often easier than following a printed pattern when you know how; you don't need to plough through pages of written instructions for one thing. You can even design as you go along if you prefer, changing your mind as you knit, according to the effects you wish to create.

So if it's so easy, why do most knitters feel lost without a pattern? Unfortunately, until recently most British patterns made it difficult for knitters to understand how pattern shapes were constructed. Faced with lengthy, row by row written instructions without a diagram or detailed measurement in sight, even many experienced knitters often had no idea how to adapt patterns to suit themselves. Yet although our pattern format is slowly improving at last, many knitters now resist the change because they have never learnt how to think for themselves when knitting.

I aim to show you the many advantages of approaching your knitting creatively, trying out different stitches, yarns, textures, colours and shapes, so you understand how interesting effects are achieved and then what you can do with them. Soon you will realize that you have become a thinking knitter at last, in complete creative control of your knitting, and free to make changes whenever you please.

Don't let limited knitting skills hold you back either. Keen beginners learn quickly with this approach because they have no preconceived ideas about following patterns, but start with an open mind and a willingness to try something new. This is all you need to start knitting your own designs almost immediately. Designing knitted garments should be fun, so don't let yourself get bogged down with technicalities. Dip into the book for a few ideas to get you started, then pick up your needles and start knitting!

Note on patterns and tension

Patterns are graded in order of difficulty as follows:

easy

average

knitter with some experience

very experienced knitter

● N.B. Garment size—figures in brackets refer to larger sizes (metric and imperial measurements given). Where only one set of measurements is given, this applies to all sizes.

● Either metric or imperial measurements should be followed throughout. For ease of use, figures given after conversion are not always exact equivalents.

Tension—it is very important to check your tension by knitting a tension square. The number of stitches and rows to 10 cm (4″.) must match that given in the pattern or the finished garment will end up too large or too small. Adjust needle sizes if necessary. (See Chapter 14 for more information.)

Terminology	
UK	*US*
cast off	bind off
stocking stitch	stockinette stitch
tension	gauge
work straight	work even
50 g	$1\frac{3}{4}$ oz approx

Knitting needle conversion table

Metric	*US*	*Old UK*
2 mm	0	14
$2\frac{1}{4}$ mm	1	13
$2\frac{1}{2}$ mm		
$2\frac{3}{4}$ mm	2	12
3 mm	2	11
$3\frac{1}{4}$ mm	3	10
$3\frac{1}{2}$ mm	4	
$3\frac{3}{4}$ mm	5	9
4 mm	6	8
$4\frac{1}{2}$ mm	7	7
5 mm	8	6
$5\frac{1}{2}$ mm	9	5
6 mm	10	4
$6\frac{1}{2}$ mm	$10\frac{1}{2}$	3
7 mm		2
$7\frac{1}{2}$ mm		1
8 mm	11	0
9 mm	13	00
10 mm	15	000

Guide to Yarn Substitution

The availability of many fashion yarns changes so quickly nowadays that specific brand names are only mentioned where they may help you identify the type of yarn required. Anyway, the whole purpose of this book is to encourage you to be creative and use your initiative when selecting yarns.

The following yarn descriptions or symbols are used in all patterns to describe the general weight and type of yarn used and give an approximate indication of the correct yarn thickness. Photographs of the actual yarns used for one pattern are included to help you select a comparable yarn substitute, together with length measurements per ball where known, as this gives a far more accurate guide to the quantity of yarn needed when selecting a substitute. (This information is included on many ball bands.)

British yarn symbols

☐1	3 ply
☐2	4 ply
☐3	Double knitting (D.K.)
☐4	Aran weight
☐5	Chunky weight
☐6	Extra chunky weight
☆☆	mohair or mohair type yarn
ø	bouclé or bouclé-type yarn
øø	fine chenille
øøø	chunky chenille
○	metallic yarn
⊗	contains metallic strands
■	slubbed yarn
★—	novelty yarn with combination of yarn types
★★	ribbon, tape or cord
☒	bi, multi-coloured or variegated yarn

American equivalents

fine weight
lightweight
medium weight
medium-heavy weight
bulky weight
extra bulky weight

Average stitch tension (over st st)

yarn type	needle size	stitches per 10 cm/4″
2 ply	2 mm–3 mm	33 + sts
3 ply	$2\frac{3}{4}$ mm–$3\frac{3}{4}$ mm	29–32
4 ply	3 mm–4 mm	25–28
Double knitting	$3\frac{1}{4}$ mm–$4\frac{1}{2}$ mm	21–24
Aran weight	$4\frac{1}{2}$ mm–$5\frac{1}{2}$ mm	17–20
Chunky	$5\frac{1}{2}$ mm–$6\frac{1}{2}$ mm	13–16
Extra chunky	$6\frac{1}{2}$ mm +	9–12

Abbreviations

alt	– alternate(ly)		psso	– pass slipped stitch over (p 33)
approx	– approximate(ly)		rem	– remain(ing)
av	– average		rep	– repeat
B	– back		rev st st	– reverse stocking stitch (p 29, 30)
beg	– begin(ning)		R	– right
CB	– centre back		RH	– right hand
CF	– centre front		RS	– right side
cm	– centimetre(s)		skpo	– slip 1, knit 1, pass slipped stitch over (p 33)
col	– colour		sk2po	– slip 1, knit 2 together, pass slipped stitch over (p 34)
cont	– continu(e)(ing)			
dec	– decreas(e)(ing) (p32–34)		sl	– slip
dble ptd	– double pointed		s1K	– slip 1 knitwise
DK	– double knitting		s1P	– slip 1 purlwise
F	– front		ssk	– slip, slip, knit (p 33)
foll	– follow(s)(ing)		st(s)	– stitch(es)
g	– gram(s)		st st	– stocking stitch (p 29, 30)
g st	– garter stitch (p 29)		tbl	– through back of loop(s) (p 33)
in	– inch(es)		tog	– together
inc	– increas(e)(ing) (p 32, 33)		WS	– wrong side
K	– knit		wyib	– with yarn in back
Kwise	– insert needle as if to knit		wyif	– with yarn in front
L	– left		yb	– yarn back (p 32)
LH	– left hand		yf	– yarn forward (p 32)
m1	– make 1 st (p 32, 33)		yon	– yarn over needle (p 32)
mb	– make bobble (p 44, 46)		yrn	– yarn round needle (p 32)
MC	– main colour		(......)	– repeat instructions inside rackets as many times as indicated after brackets
mm	– millimetre(s)			
No(s)	– number(s)			
oz	– ounce(s)		*......*	– repeat instructions from or between asterisk(s)
P	– purl			
patt	– pattern			
Pwise	– insert needle as if to purl			

Section 1
TEXTURE

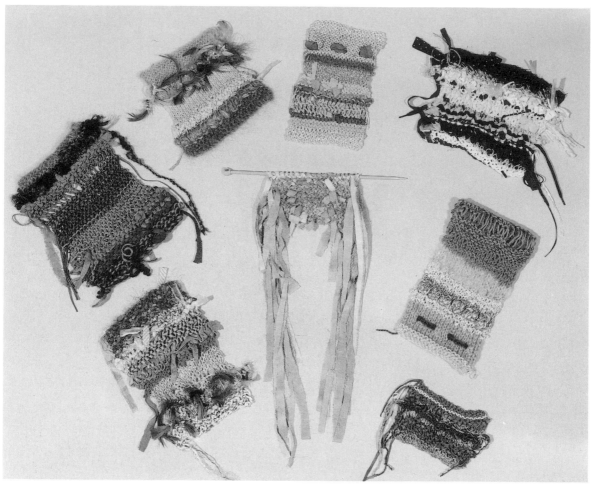

1 Experimental samples using yarn alternatives. Knitted by (from top left working clockwise) Pauline Knight, Dilys McIntyre, Frieda Oxenham, Kate Sendles, Jan Pattinson, Marie Holmes, Alison Jabs, (centre) Marie Holmes

1
Loosen up and relax

Presumably you like knitting or you wouldn't have bothered to open up this book. But you may not have thought about knitting your own designs before, or if you have, you probably didn't know where to begin. So we're going to start by trying out a few experiments to encourage you to break away from conventional ideas about hand-knitting yarns and texture. At the same time you will find that you will begin to loosen up and relax, and before long you will be ready to start introducing a few ideas of your own. (Complete beginners should read Chapter 4 first, for how to cast on and knit basic garter stitch.)

First, gather together a selection of rather unusual things to knit with. Here are some suggestions:

string, shoelaces, leather thonging, ribbon, cotton, tape, bias binding, Christmas tinsel, braid, lace edging, raffia, piping cord, thin wire, fishing line, polythene strip, nylon twine, ric rac, laddered tights and fabric cut into strips.

Perhaps you can think of some more—the crazier the better!

Choose one of these yarn alternatives and cast on about 20 stitches, using a pair of any large size knitting needles (size 6½ mm or bigger). Start knitting in garter stitch, stocking stitch or any other stitch you fancy. Change to something different after a few rows—you may run out of things like shoelaces pretty soon anyway! Join on a new yarn with a knot wherever it happens to fall, even on the right side in the middle of a row if you like, it really doesn't matter. Technique is completely irrelevant at this stage; it's the effect you're after, and all those knots are probably already starting to make you feel

quite bold and daring. See—you are beginning to break conventional rules, even at this stage!

After about 10 cm (4 in.), sit back and look at what you've got. You may find that apart from loosening up your conventional ideas about what knitting should look like, you may already have produced that gem of an idea for your first design in knitted texture. If not, try again with a different combination of needle size, stitch and 'yarn'; you

2 Knitted samples using string, bias binding, raffia and fabric strips

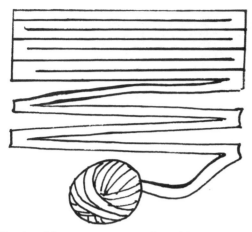

3 Cutting fabric strips—1 cm ($\frac{1}{2}$″) width strips

will be bound to turn up with something you like before long.

Incidentally, don't throw away any of your sample squares at this stage; what you first thought of as a disaster may prove to be very useful later on as your ideas progress. Remember, these aren't boring old tension squares, they are possible test samples for your future designs. But they do act as a record for your tension too. So, before you forget, buy a pack of string labelling tags from your local stationers, make a note of what size needles you used and tie the information on to each sample for future reference. They make your samples look much more professional too—an important point at this early stage when all you have to show for your efforts is a pile of strange little squares of knotted knitting without a finished sweater in sight.

DROPPED STITCHES

What to do if you don't know how to pick them up again

Don't pull the knitting off the needles in frustration—see page 30 for the answer or make a feature of the dropped stitches instead! Beginners soon discover that a dropped stitch turns into a ladder running downwards, leaving a line of loose floating threads in its wake. Thread a piece of ribbon or fancy yarn through the dropped stitch together with the bar immediately above it, and finish with a knot or bow to anchor the stitch firmly.

4 Wallhanging made from coloured tights and metallic yarn

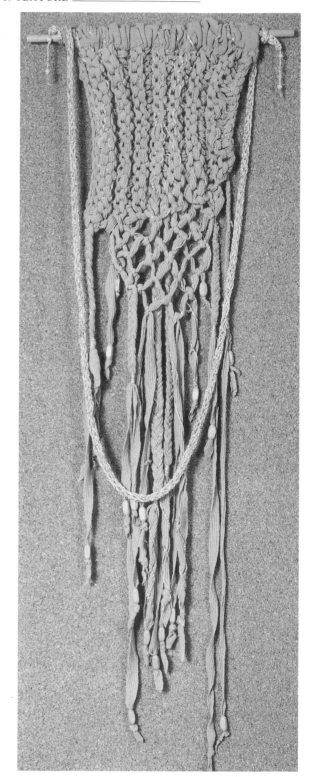

14

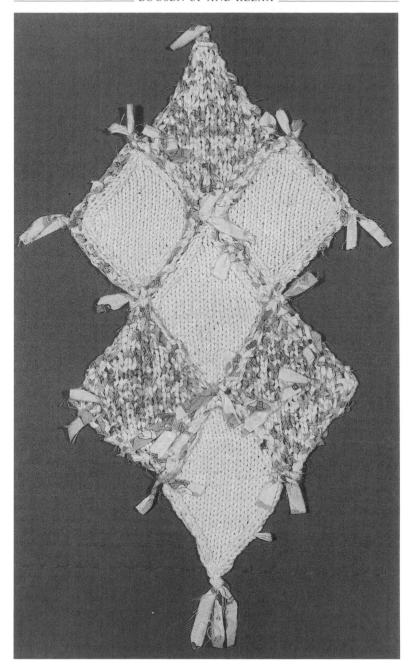

5 Wallhanging made from cotton yarn and fabric strips

Tie on a few more bows here and there—even drop another ladder or two if you dare! Then decorate the ladder(s) by weaving raffia, shoelaces or whatever you like through the gaps. Alternatively, leave the ladders bare for a see-through effect. With luck, your disaster will turn into a striking design feature. No one will guess how it happened, so just smile sweetly amidst all the compliments!

15

Pattern Project 1

Rag knitted bag

Materials

200–300 g of assorted yarn alternatives and fabric cut into strips about 1 cm ($\frac{1}{2}''$) wide.
1 pair 10 mm (US 15) needles

To work

For a bag about 30–40 cm (12–16″) wide:
Using fabric strips knotted together to form a continuous length of yarn, cast on 25–30 sts and work straight in any stitch you like, e.g., garter stitch.

Continue until work measures double the length you require for finished bag (60–80 cm (24–32″)).
Cast off.

MAKING UP

Fold bag in half, and knit, stitch or crochet the sides together.
Add a length of french knitting, or a twisted or

6 Rag knitted bag (variation)

plaited cord at each side of top edge to make a strap (see Chapter 7).
Decorate with beads, tassels or fringing.
Adapt this idea for cushions and simple rectangular tops, or use the photographs shown in this chapter to help you with ideas for making other simple starter projects.

Pattern Project 2

Rag knitted jacket

See colour section
Measurements
To fit bust 81–96 cm/32–38″.
Finished length from shoulder to hem 58 cm/23″.

Materials
Total finished weight of jacket 550 g approx, made up of fabric strips, doubled DK cotton yarn, ribbon and bias binding.

Add assorted yarns and yarn alternatives of your own choosing.
1 pair size 8 mm (US 11) & size 10 mm (US 15) needles.

Tension
8 sts & 10 rows to 10 cm/4″ approx in patt on size 10 mm needles.

Abbreviations—See page 10.

MAIN BODY

(starting at lower back edge)
Cast on 36 sts with size 8 mm needles and work in K1, P1 rib for 6 cm (2$\frac{1}{2}$″).
Change to size 10 mm needles and (K8, inc 1) 4 times (40 sts).

7 Rag knitted jacket measurement diagram and visual pattern. Compare this with written row by row instructions and see how much easier it is to understand when presented visually (full details in shaping section).

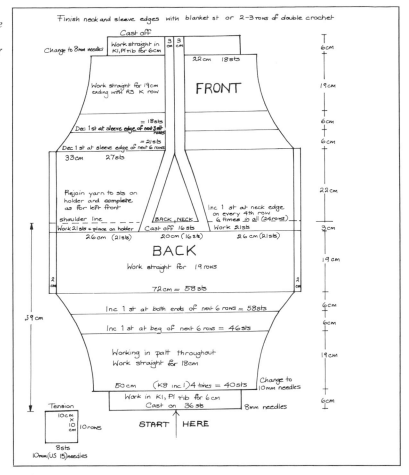

Finish neck and sleeve edges with blanket st or 2-3 rows of double crochet

Cast off

Change to 8mm needles — Work straight in K1, P1 rib for 6cm — 3 cm · 3 cm — 6cm

22cm 18sts

FRONT — 19cm

Work straight for 19cm ending with RS K row

= 18sts — 6cm
Dec 1st at sleeve edge of next 3 alt rows
= 21sts — 6cm
Dec 1st at sleeve edge of next 6 rows
33cm 27sts

Inc 1st at neck edge on every 4th row 6 times in all (24 rows) — 22cm

Rejoin yarn to sts on holder and complete as for left front

shoulder line _ _ _ _
Work 21 sts + place on holder — BACK, NECK Cast off 16 sts — Work 21sts — 3cm
26cm (21sts) 20cm (16sts) 26cm (21sts)

BACK — 19cm

Work straight for 19 rows

72cm = 58sts

2 cm — Inc 1st at both ends of next 6 rows = 58sts — 6cm

Inc 1st at beg of next 6 rows = 46sts — 6cm

.59cm — Working in patt throughout Work straight for 18cm — 19cm

50cm (K8 inc 1) 4 times = 40sts — Change to 10mm needles

Work in K1, P1 rib for 6cm — 8mm needles — 6cm
Cast on 36 sts

START | HERE

Tension
10cm
x
10
cm | 10 rows

8sts
10mm (US 15) needles

Work in patt as follows, changing col and yarn every 2 rows approx.

Rows 1 & 3 Knit.

Rows 2 & 4 Purl.

Row 5 (sl 1, K1) rep to end of row.

Row 6 Purl.

Row 7 (K1, yf) rep to last st, K1.

Row 8 (P1, yrn, drop extra yf loops) rep to last st, P1.

Row 9 K, dropping all extra loops.

Row 10 Purl.

Rep patt rows 1–10 throughout.

Cont straight until 18 cm (7″) of patt have been worked, ending with WS row.

Inc 1 st at beg of next 6 rows (46 sts).

Inc 1 st at both ends of next 6 rows (58 sts).

Work straight for 19 rows.

Next row WS Divide for neck: work 21 sts and slip onto spare needle, cast off 16 sts, work to end. Cont on last 21 sts.

Inc 1 st at neck edge on every 4th row, 6 times in all (27 sts).

Dec 1 st at sleeve edge of next 6 rows (21 sts).

Dec 1 st at sleeve edge of next 3 alt rows (18 sts).

Work straight for 19 cm (7½″), ending with a RS row.

Change to size 8 mm needles and work in K1, P1, rib for 6 cm (2½″). Cast off.

With RS facing, rejoin yarn to sts on needle at neck edge. Complete to match right front.

MAKING UP

Join side seams. Neaten neck and sleeve openings with blanket st or 2–3 rows of double crochet.

2

Finding ideas to inspire you

One of the first questions I am often asked is where do I get all my ideas? People never fail to be surprised when I tell them some of the huge variety of unlikely sources which have inspired me over the years—anything from spiders' webs to brick walls to knotted tree trunks! It all boils down to being constantly aware and ever open to new possibilities by observing what you see around you every day, and thinking how you could use interesting textures, shapes, patterns and colour combinations as inspiration for design projects. However, concentrate on the rather more obvious design sources to begin with—that is, those that relate directly to knitting.

OLD KNITTING BOOKS AND PATTERNS

Begin by keeping your eyes open for old knitting books from the 20s, 30s, 40s and 50s at jumble sales, house clearances and second hand bookshops, or ask any elderly knitters you know if they still have any old knitting patterns tucked away in the loft or under the stairs. If they are keen knitters now, they probably have been for many years, and they may be only too pleased to dig out old patterns for you if you show an interest. Sift through them all, and amongst the quaint, old fashioned, and sometimes frankly bizarre styles of the past you should be able to spot an unfamiliar but interesting neckline here, an unusual combination of stitches there, or sometimes even a complete design which is just right for today when knitted up in the latest yarns with all their kaleidoscopic varieties of colour and texture.

Many up and coming knitwear designers do precisely this when they are first starting out. If you

look carefully you may well stumble across the sources of inspiration for quite a few of today's styles. When you've found an old pattern with modern design potential, then it is simply a matter of substituting modern yarns for those no longer being manufactured.

YARN SUBSTITUTION

Pre-war patterns usually specified much finer yarns than those around today. In fact, double knitting and chunky yarns were not really widely available until the late 50s so you'll probably be restricted to using 2, 3 and 4 ply yarns; indeed, you may not recognize some of the old discontinued yarn brand names anyway. However, if you check the needle sizes specified in the pattern you can gain a basic idea of the original yarn weight and thickness in order to make an intelligent substitute choice, even if the ply isn't actually mentioned. The charts on pages 8 and 9 will also help to guide you.

For instance, old British or imperial size 10 and size 12 needles indicate that the pattern will probably be suitable for an average modern 4 ply yarn, knitted with size 12 needles (equivalent metric size $2\frac{3}{4}$ mm) for the rib or welt section, and size 10 ($3\frac{1}{4}$ mm) for the main body and sleeve sections. Yarns of 2 and 3 ply weight are also frequently specified in old patterns, and these are much less widely available today because most modern knitters demand yarns which can be knitted up quickly. Lack of patience—particularly among younger knitters—is undoubtedly a contributory factor too! However, now that fitted styles are back in fashion again, demand for finer, smoother yarns is likely to return.

However, finer yarns *are* still available if you know where to look (see specialist yarn suppliers at the back of the book); you can still purchase even 1 ply yarn if you've always yearned to make one of those beautiful knitted lace 'ring' shawls (so called because traditionally their fineness was judged on whether they could be pulled through a wedding ring). Incidentally, do remember that 2 ply shetland wool yarn is actually equivalent in thickness to most branded 4 ply knitting yarns, and 'lace' weight shetland yarns are equivalent to most 2–3 ply weight yarns.

DESIGN SOURCES AND ITEMS OF KNITTING INTEREST

The next thing to do is to start a reference file on all aspects of knitting which interest you, for example:

magazine and press cuttings of designer knits
features on knitwear designers—their approach to their work and methods of designing
favourite patterns
knitting hints and tips
history of knitting

Look out for ideas and resources—that is, anything at all which might inspire your future designs. Start collecting postcards and magazine cuttings of pictures which include interesting colours, textures, shapes or patterns. You will soon discover that such items as impressionist paintings, ethnic and oriental costume, stained glass windows, mosaics, decorative wall tiles, geographic features, rock strata, aerial photographs or flora and fauna of all kinds will all provide an endless source of inspiration if you study them closely. (See how in Chapter 13.)

I also like to add a section for yarn samples I have used and liked (or hated!) tying a short length of yarn to the relevant ball band so I remember the details of each one for possible use later.

Incidentally, did you know that a wealth of useful information is printed on most ball bands? Most people never look beyond the brand name, but the small print also tells you the recommended size of knitting or crochet needle for that yarn, together with the average tension achieved—that is, the average number of stitches and rows needed to knit up a 10 cm (4″) square. The composition of the yarn will be mentioned too, together with the percentage of each fibre used in the make up, and, of course, the shade or colour code number and dye lot. The country of origin will usually be specified as well, and also washing, pressing and dry cleaning instructions are given.

MAIL ORDER YARN SUPPLIERS

Finally, if you don't live within easy reach of a good yarn stockist it is a good idea to scour the small ads in knitting and craft magazines and send off for yarn samples and shade cards. The number of mail order yarn suppliers has mushroomed in recent years, owing to the boom in popularity of fashion knitting. Many firms now specialize in unusual yarns in a wide range of colours. A small charge is usually made for sending samples, which is frequently deducted from any future orders you send to the firm in question. Every preference is catered for, from luxurious silks, cashmere, alpaca, mohair and angora; to sturdy shetlands, arans and oiled wools from the hardy breeds of sheep; as well as fancy textured yarns such as chenille, slub, bouclé and brushed yarns. And of course nowadays a wide range of cotton yarns is available for summer

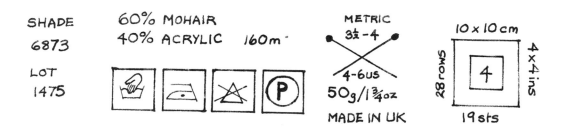

8 Ballband information

9 Sources of inspiration

knitting. (A small selection of specialist yarn suppliers is included on pages 155, 156.)

ORGANIZING A KNITTING REFERENCE FILE

You will probably start off by tucking your snippets of information into your knitting bag, or throwing them loose into a spare drawer. But as the pile grows, it is well worth the time spent sorting them out and clipping them into a ring back file or document folder with divider headings such as *Patterns, Technical tips, Designer cuttings, Shade cards,* etc., so you know exactly where to find information when you need it.

You may prefer to keep sample shade cards in a shoe box or something similar. They are often very bulky and tend to take up too much space in a file. It is also easier to mix and match yarns from different suppliers if they are kept loose, so you can easily move them around in order to check one shade against another.

In addition, A4 size transparent plastic envelopes with holes punched down one side (available from large stationers) keep your magazine cuttings and patterns wonderfully neat and tidy. They look professional too. The only trouble is that if, like me you tend to get carried away with enthusiasm, one file soon becomes two, then three or four, and before long you've got a whole bookshelf of files! But I wouldn't be without mine for anything—they are lovingly crammed full of fascinating information which I have amassed over the years and refer to constantly—and what a marvellous source of inspiration they prove to be whenever I am stuck for ideas!

3
All about needles and yarn

NEEDLES

Before you can start knitting, you will need to buy yourself at least one pair of needles. Experienced knitters often own large numbers of knitting needles in a range of different sizes and types to cope with particular knitting processes. But until you know whether you're going to enjoy knitting, one or two pairs are quite sufficient to learn the basic skills, so the initial outlay on equipment is very small.

Which needles to choose? The choice may look rather confusing at first, but if you're new to knitting you'll almost certainly start off with flat knitting, working from side to side in separate rows, for which you'll need a *pair of needles* which have a point at one end and a knob at the other to stop the stitches slipping off. The size of needle used varies according to the thickness of the yarn—generally speaking, the thicker the yarn the wider the needle diameter. A guide to needle sizes with suggested appropriate yarn weights is given on page 8.

Double knitting weight yarn is the most widely available yarn quality nowadays, and usually looks best knitted up on needles that are approximately size 4 mm. Each needle size is also available in several lengths, chosen according to personal preference and the type and size of garment you want to make. Modern needles in coated aluminium, plastic, wood and bamboo are all light and easy to use, but you may find you prefer the handle of one type of needle to another.

If you wish to knit 'in the round' without seams, you will also need a *set of four (or 5) needles* with points at both ends for smaller items like socks, hats and gloves. Three of the needles are used to hold the stitches in a triangular shape, with the fourth used

to knit each set of stitches in turn, continuing round and round to form a circular tube that is comfortable to wear and eliminates the bother of sewing up seams. A full range of sizes is available.

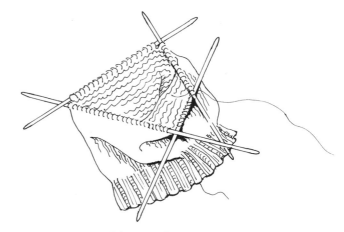

12 Knitting on set of four needles

Circular needles are used for knitting in rounds when there are too many stitches to fit onto a set of four needles. They are made up of two needles linked by a piece of flexible plastic and are available in 40, 60, 80 or 100 cm (16, 24, 35, 39″) lengths for each size. The total needle length must be shorter than the circle to be knitted so they are not suitable for small numbers of stitches. They can also be used for knitting to and fro and are particularly useful for heavy weight knits, since the bulk of the weight is carried on the knitter's lap, instead of hanging from the working ends of the needles. They are also

10 *Assorted types of needles and knitting equipment*

11 *Key to knitting equipment*

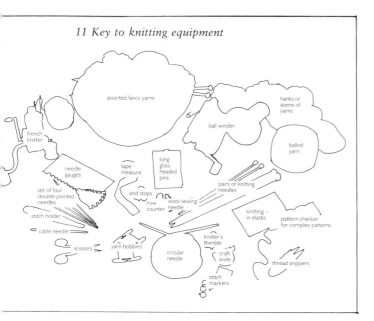

assorted fancy yarns

hanks or
skeins of
yarns

french
knitter

ball winder

balled
yarn

needle
gauges

tape
measure

long
glass
headed
pins

set of four
double-pointed
needles

pairs of knitting
needles

end stops

wool sewing
needle

row
counter

knitting –
in elastic

pattern checker
for complex patterns

stitch holder

cable needle

scissors

yarn bobbins

circular
needle

knitter's
thimble

craft
knife

thread snippers

stitch
markers

useful for knitting on journeys as they are compact and less likely to jab into your neighbour.

Later on, you may also need one or two *cable needles* for crossover cable patterns. These needles are short and double pointed.

Stitch holders resemble large safety pins and are used when you divide the working stitches into two or more sections. One group of stitches is knitted up first, leaving the remainder on a stitch holder to be knitted up at a later stage.

A *needle gauge* is useful for measuring double pointed and circular needles which have no size marked on them. Various other optional, cheap and handy knitting gadgets are available, such as *row counters and ring markers*, which are threaded onto the needles to keep track of stitches and rows knitted, and *end stops*, which prevent stitches coming off between knitting sessions. *Yarn bobbins* help with patchwork blocks of colour knitting.

Last, but not least, a *wool sewing needle* with a

22

large eye and blunt point is essential for finishing off your work and sewing up seams. A crochet hook is useful too and a tape measure, ruler, scissors and pins (long glass-headed ones are best) will also be necessary. Don't buy expensive, specialist items like a *ball winder* and *knitting swift* – which holds and rotates skeins of yarn to facilitate fast winding – unless you plan to use large quantities of skeined yarn.

YARNS

Next you must decide on some yarn. This need not be expensive—most knitting shops have a rummage bin of yarn oddments left over from last season's lines which are sold at greatly reduced prices in order to make way for new stock. Choose a ball of plain, smooth, approximately double knitting weight yarn in any colour which takes your fancy so you can practise the basic stitches.

Yarns vary so enormously nowadays in appearance, handle, price and fibre content, so it is wise to know a little about the various yarn classifications.

Fibres
Natural fibres are obtained from animals or plants. Cotton and linen are of plant origin, whereas wool, mohair, angora, alpaca, cashmere, vicuna, camel hair and silk come from animals. Some of these fibres are difficult to obtain and are therefore much more expensive to buy in yarn form.

Modern technology has also produced a large range of *man-made* fibres, for example, viscose rayon, nylon, acrylic and polyester. Viscose rayon is a cellulose fibre derived from wood pulp, whereas all the others are true synthetics produced from mineral sources. Unlikely raw materials such as coal, petrol and oil products are chemically processed into liquid form and forced through a tiny hole called a spinneret.

The liquid solidifies on reaching the air, and forms long, continuous filament threads. This imitates the natural production of silk by the silkworm, which emits a continuous filament of silk through an orifice in its head in a similar manner. Sometimes the filaments are cut up into short staple lengths, which are then combed, drawn and spun into staple yarns in much the same way as natural fibres.

Man-made fibres are machine-washable, strong, shrinkproof and cheap to produce; however, they do not 'breathe' or have the same warmth, handle or resilience as natural fibres. So new blends are constantly being developed to combine the advantages of both natural and man-made fibres more successfully. In fact, man-made fibre yarns often resemble natural fibres so closely in appearance that it is wise to check ball bands carefully for fibre content and washing instructions in order to avoid mistakes.

Personally, I still feel that natural fibres are hard to beat for appearance and comfort in wear. But I simply cannot resist also using many of the new fancy textured fashion yarns because of their enormous visual and tactile appeal.

Ply
Ply is the name given to a single spun thread, which can be of any thickness. Two or more plys are then twisted together in various ways to give yarns of recognized thickness and strength. However, not all yarns of the same ply are necessarily the same thickness. For example, some shetland yarns have a 2 ply construction but, confusingly, are as thick as most 4 ply yarns.

However, on the whole, *2, 3 and 4 ply* weights are generally used to describe classic, smooth yarns of a recognized thickness. *Double knitting* has a 4 ply construction, but produces a thicker fabric because each ply is roughly double the thickness of those used in an average 4 ply knitting yarn. Aran weight is roughly three times the thickness of 4 ply yarn. *Chunky and double double knittings* are double the thickness of double knitting yarns and are mainly used for outdoor garments.

Speciality and novelty effect yarns
Yarns in this category—such as, bouclé, chenille, lurex, mohair, ribbons, slubbed and knopped yarns—have made an enormous impact on the knitting scene recently. They have a decorative appearance and include those with a fancy texture, which is often achieved by combining plain and textured plys from different fibre groups, or by twisting plys together unevenly. Fashion yarns are often expensive, but are nevertheless highly popular and sell well because of their great visual appeal; they are also attractive to handle and have eye-catching novelty value.

Ball weights, hanks and skeins
Most yarns nowadays are sold in ready wound balls of 20, 25, 40, 50 or 100 gm in weight. Check the weight carefully on the ball band when comparing

13 Yarn fibres, weights and types

prices, as an apparently cheap 20 gm ball may actually cost more gram for gram than a slightly pricier 25 gm ball. A few yarns are still sold in hanks or skeins—these need to be wound into balls ready for use.

It would be helpful if the length in metres per ball were also stated more often, as a lightweight fine yarn will go a lot further than a ball of similar weight in heavier, thick yarn.

Using yarns to best advantage

The use of different types of yarns can change the appearance and character of a piece of knitting out of all recognition. If you choose one stitch you like and knit up a sample in four entirely different yarns you will see what I mean for yourself.

Try out any favourite stitch pattern knitted in plain double knit wool, cotton chenille, bouclé and mohair and you will see how the plainer wool yarn shows up the stitch formation clearly, whereas the fancier textured yarns tend to hide the stitches. The obvious conclusion to be drawn from this is to use smooth uncomplicated yarns for fancy stitch patterns and save your fancy textured yarns for plain simple knitting. There is absolutely no point in wasting precious time knitting complicated stitches which will not be clearly seen.

This is one reason why fancy yarns have been so successful, as they give inexperienced knitters the opportunity to create beautiful knitted garments without being highly skilled. They are often suitable for knitting on large needles and therefore popular with most knitters with busy lifestyles.

Yet, often, you may have tried knitting a jumper using one of the most gorgeous fancy textured yarns you've ever laid eyes on, only to feel that the yarn looked nicer in the ball than when knitted up. Somehow it often loses something during the knitting process. To avoid such disappointment I now use small amounts only of fancy yarns, mixed in with several plain ones, so that maximum impact is gained from each. In this way the eye alights on each area of texture in turn, discovering the more obvious ones first, then progressing to the more subtle, pausing to take in nuances of colour and stitch along the way. Thus, the merits of the garment are fully appreciated and inwardly digested before the eye finally moves on to something else.

Try these texture ideas yourself, before learning to combine colours in Section 2 and putting together simple shapes in Section 3.

4
Stitches and the very basics

Knitting can be as simple or as complicated as you wish, but however intricate the stitch, there are only four basic procedures to learn. All other stitches are only variations or combinations of the following:

- casting on
- plain (knit)
- purl
- casting off

HOLDING YOUR NEEDLES

There are several different ways you can choose to hold your needles. These differences tend to be regionally based, and also depend on whether short or long needles are being used. One needle is held in each hand, the right hand needle being used to hold new stitches, with the left hand holding the completed stitches and resting on top of the work with a relaxed overhand grip. If you are left handed, life becomes more complicated as usual, and you will need to reverse all the instructions. It is probably easiest to prop the diagrams up in front of a mirror and work from the reflection.

The so called *English method* requires the yarn to be held in the right hand, but there are two alternative ways of holding the right hand needle. Knitters in the south of England use an *underhand grip*, as if holding a pencil. My mother taught me this method in childhood and like most knitters I have stuck to the method which I find most familiar. It is difficult to force oneself to change anyway, even though I now realize it is far from being the fastest way to knit. This particular grip is generally thought to have originated in Victorian times when knitting at last became acceptable as a drawing room pastime suitable for ladies. Knitting speed and efficiency was of no importance to this new class of knitters, so a more refined way of holding the needles was contrived purely for the sake of elegance—similar to crooking the little finger while drinking a cup of tea.

This was far from being the case in many areas of the north of England, Scotland and the Shetland Isles, in particular, where the rural population often relied on the cottage knitting industries as a way of making ends meet and keeping their families warm. This is why knitters from the north still use the more efficient *double overhand grip*, which gives greater

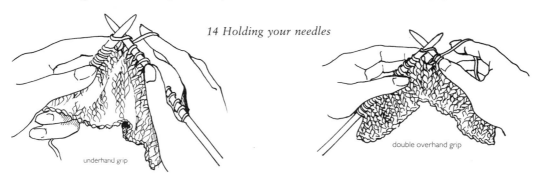

14 Holding your needles

underhand grip

double overhand grip

25

speed and control over the work, a method also used in Spain. Energy and time are saved by anchoring the right-hand needle under the arm or tucking it into a belt or specially made knitting sheath to keep it steady, while the left-hand needle alone copes with all the movement. The right hand is then free to concentrate on feeding the yarn. Long needles are therefore more appropriate for this method, even when using relatively small numbers of stitches, although shorter double-pointed needles are also suitable if used in conjunction with a belt or sheath.

Knitters from the south tend to prefer short needles, because if the right needle is not anchored the ends of long needles wave around more and get in the way. Circular needles are also comfortable to use and have been popularized, in particular, by the designer Kaffe Fassett.

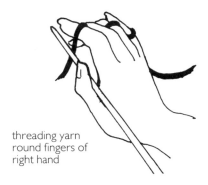

threading yarn
round fingers of
right hand

Both handling methods use the right forefinger to throw the yarn around the tip of the right-hand needles, which is the critical movement for regulating knitting tension. Beginners often let go of the right-hand needle to achieve this, which not only wastes time but is bound to cause uneven tension. However, if the yarn is first wound round the fingers of the right hand so that the index finger can control the flow of yarn evenly under tension *while still gripping the needle*, there is no need to let go, and the knitting progresses much more quickly and evenly. It may take a little longer to master this movement, but the effort taken will be repaid a thousand times over.

The *continental method* differs from the English method in that the yarn is carried in the left hand. Both hands are held on top of the needles with the butt ends allowed to move freely, so it is best to use the shortest possible needles for the number of stitches to be worked, or alternatively, circular needles. The right needle hooks the yarn from the

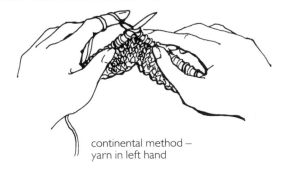

continental method –
yarn in left hand

left-hand forefinger, which involves the right wrist in a good deal of movement. Its undoubted speed in use is counteracted by the fact that it can sometimes prove difficult to maintain the same tension for both knit and purl stitches. It is worth learning how to knit with both right- and left-hand methods as you will find it a great advantage when learning how to cope with multi-colour knitting techniques.

CASTING ON

Casting on is always the first step in knitting and forms a foundation row of loops on the needle. It can be done in a number of different ways, but I have found most people again stick to the method they learn first, only changing tack when a pattern particularly specifies an alternative method. Complete beginners should look at the first two methods outlined here, and choose whichever looks the easier. Try the other methods later as and when you need them. *The Handknitters Handbook* by Montse Stanley (David & Charles, 1986), shows about 40 different methods and variations of casting on—a must for reference purposes.

Using smooth plain yarn, practise the basic stitches as follows:

Making a slip knot to start
Make a slip knot about 10 cm (4″) from the end of a ball of yarn by winding the yarn twice around two fingers so the strands cross over each other. Then pull a loop through the twisted yarn with a knitting needle, pulling both ends of the yarn to tighten the slip knot.

Casting on—two needle cable method
This gives a strong, firm, rope-like, general purpose edge with some elasticity.

1 Hold needle with slip knot in your left hand, gripping end of yarn firmly.

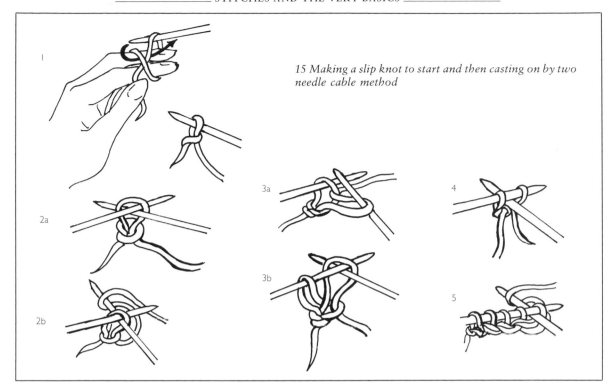

15 Making a slip knot to start and then casting on by two needle cable method

2 Insert the right hand (RH) needle through slip loop from front to back and wind the yarn under and over RH needle.

3 Draw new loop through slip loop to make st and place on left hand (LH) needle by twisting as shown. Withdraw RH needle.

4 3rd and succeeding sts—insert RH needle between last 2 loops on LH needle and wind yarn under and over RH needle again. Draw through new loop and place on LH needle as before.

5 Continue in this way until you have cast on required number of sts.

(A looser edge can be formed by inserting RH needle *through* last st on LH needle from front to back each time, instead of *between* last 2 sts)

Casting on—one needle thumb method
This method produces a hard wearing but elastic edge.

1 Make a slip knot and place on needle as before, this time leaving an end about 1 metre (1 yd) long for every 100 to be cast on. Hold needle in RH.

16 Casting on—one needle thumb method/single loop cast on/casting on—invisible

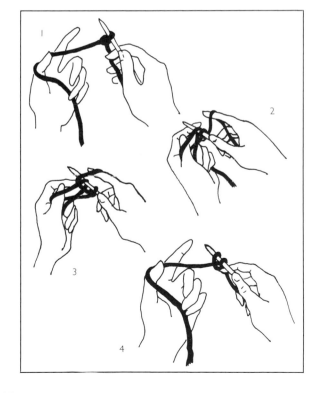

2 Wind shorter end of yarn around L thumb clockwise as shown, holding it taut across palm with last three fingers. Insert RH needle under front of loop on thumb.

3 Wind the ball end of yarn round needle with R forefinger. Then draw it through thumb loop to make new st. Tighten both ends of yarn.

4 Cont in this way until you have cast on required No. of sts.

Single loop cast on—one needle thumb method

This method is very loose and light, and is therefore suitable for lacy or fine knitting. It is also recommended as a temporary cast on method when the cast on stitches have to be picked up and worked in the opposite direction later, since the join so formed is invisible. In this case, a contrasting yarn is used for the cast on row, which is unravelled when required to expose a row of loops which are then picked up and knitted as normal. These loops can also be grafted invisibly (see page 152) to a row of stitches from the opposite end of the knitting—for example, to form a circular border—or to stitches from another piece of knitting altogether.

Follow steps 1–2 as for previous thumb method cast on but leave only a short free end of yarn.

3 Insert RH needle under front of thumb loop and slip off onto needle, pulling yarn tight with LH.

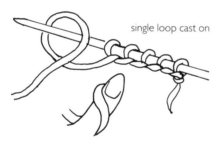

single loop cast on

4 Rep as many times as necessary to form required No. of sts.

Don't be deceived by the apparent simplicity of this cast on method. You will find that the row to follow is more difficult to knit than normal.

Casting on—invisible

This method is used purely for a temporary cast on to create an unfinished edge which can be returned to at a later stage. The yarn is wound around the needles with the aid of a foundation yarn, such as a long end from the same ball of yarn, which can then

casting on – invisible

be used like a drawstring to allow the edge to be gathered up or to stretch freely as required. Alternatively, a contrasting foundation yarn can be used, which on removal exposes a row of loops that can be picked up and knitted in the opposite direction without a visible join, just like the single loop cast on. This technique is harder to master than the previous method, but the speed and ease with which the foundation yarn can be withdrawn makes it a worthwhile alternative to the single loop cast on.

It is not suitable for beginners, and is best attempted with a contrasting foundation yarn at first to avoid confusion as to which yarn is which. (Try it, and you'll see what I mean!)

1 Make a slip knot leaving an end long enough to hold required number of sts, or use separate length of contrasting yarn.

2 Holding needle in RH, wind yarn forward under needle and foundation yarn, back over top of needle and under again.

3 Go over foundation yarn, then underneath and back over needle.

Rep steps 2 and 3 until you have cast on required No. of sts.

A specialized cast on method for rib is included in the Ribbing Section on page 31.

KNIT (PLAIN) STITCH

This is the simplest of the two basic knitting stitches, knit (plain) and purl. In knit (K) stitches the new loop is drawn through to the side of the work facing you, and forms a smooth flat stitch at the front and a bumpy ridge at the back.

1 Hold needle with sts in LH, with yarn held at back of work. Insert tip of free RH needle into 1st st Kwise (that is, from front to back) passing it under LH needle.

2 Wind yarn under and over RH needle from behind.

3 Draw new loop through st on LH needle, slipping st off LH needle.

4 New loop is now on RH needle and 1st st is completed.

5 Rep sequence until all sts are on RH needle.

You have now completed your first knit row. Notice that the knitting is flat and smooth at the front and bumpy on the other side.

6 Now transfer R needle to LH, and free needle to RH, turning work round so bumpy side of knitting faces you.

Start another row. Look at your knitting again when you have finished several rows.

You now have rows of smooth stitches interspersed by horizontal ridged rows of bumpy stitches on *both* sides of the work. Working entirely in knit stitch like this is the simplest way to make a knitted fabric, and is therefore the most suitable for beginners. It is called *garter stitch* because its sideways stretch made it particularly suitable for making garters in days gone by. It is also reversible as it looks the same on both sides of the work.

PURL STITCH

When you want to make a knitted fabric which has all the smooth rows on one side and all the ridged rows on the other side you will need to learn the

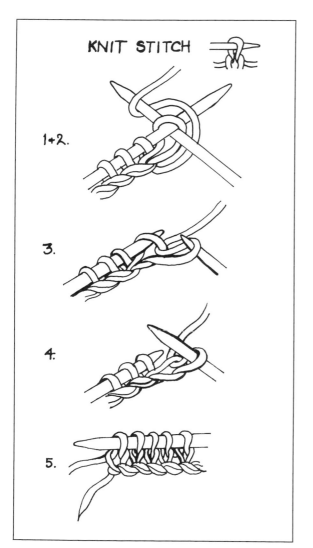

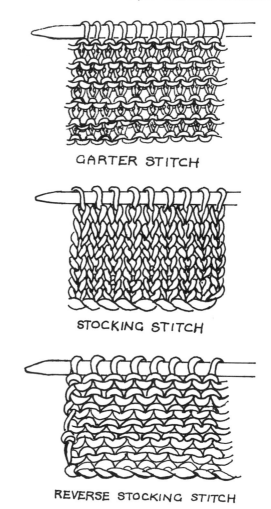

17 *Knit stitch, garter stitch, stocking stitch, reverse stocking stitch*

29

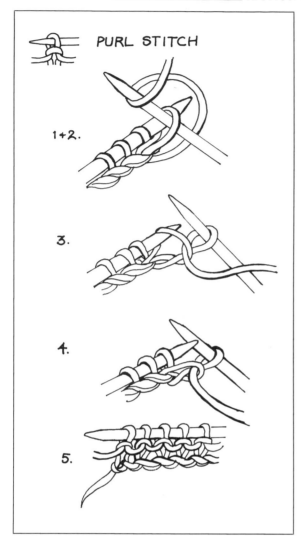

PURL STITCH

1+2.

3.

4.

5.

6 Transfer needles from one hand to another as before, ready to work another row of sts as required.

Knitting which has all the smooth textured rows on the right side of the work and all the ridges on the wrong side is called *stocking stitch*—originally because its lengthwise stretch meant that it was considered very suitable for making stockings. It is the most popular and widely used of all knitting stitches, the smooth texture being formed by knitting every right side row and purling every wrong side row. (*Reverse stocking stitch* means that the order is reversed so that purl rows are worked on the right side and knit rows on the wrong side. In this case the ridged side ends up on the right side of the work).

PICKING UP DROPPED STITCHES

With smooth side of work facing you, insert crochet hook through dropped stitch from front and draw loose strand from row above through loop as shown. Repeat process rung by rung up the ladder until the stitch is back on the needle.

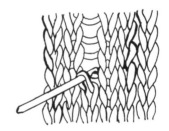

PICKING UP DROPPED STITCHES

other basic stitch, purl (P), which forms a bumpy stitch at the front and a smooth, flat stitch at the back. The new loop is drawn through to the back of the work *away* from you this time.

1 Hold needle with sts in LH, holding yarn at front. Insert tip of free RH needle into 1st st Pwise (i.e. from back to front) passing it under LH needle.
2 Wind yarn over and under needle from front.
3 Draw new loop through st on LH needle to back, slipping st off LH needle.
4 New loop is now on RH needle and first P stitch is complete.
5 Rep sequence until all sts are on RH needle. You have now completed one purl row.

RIBBING

You can also mix knit and purl stitches together in the same row to form a series of vertical 'ribs'. These produce a horizontally elastic fabric called *ribbing* which springs back into shape and clings during wear, making it ideally suitable for areas of a garment which need to stretch and grip such as cuffs, welts and necklines. Ribbing is often reversible.

Various rib patterns can be made by alternating different combinations of knit and purl stitches across the row. They have varying degrees of grip and elasticity, and are usually knitted with needles one or two sizes smaller than those used for the main stitch pattern.

Single rib

The most popular rib is *single rib*, which grips strongly and is knitted as follows:

1 Knit first st in row.
2 Bring yarn forward between needles to front of work, ready to purl.
3 Purl next st.
4 Take yarn to back of work, ready to knit.

Repeat this sequence—that is, (K1, P1) to end of row.

On next and every foll row, all the stitches which were knitted in the previous row must be purled, and all the stitches purled must be knitted, since the other side of the work is now facing you. Decide whether to knit or purl first by looking at the next stitch before you work it. If it has the flat V shape of a knit stitch at the front, then knit it. If it has the bumpy ridge of a purl stitch, purl it.

However, if you purl the knit stitches and knit the purl stitches you will produce what is known as *moss or seed stitch*. Single rib has a multiple of two stitches, so if you have an even number of stitches you will always start with a knit stitch and end with a purl stitch. With an odd number of stitches you will start and finish with a knit stitch on the first row, but a purl stitch on every alternate row.

Try and train yourself to recognize the appearance of both stitches as soon as possible. Then you can start to develop the ability to understand knitting by looking at it rather than just following pattern instructions blindly.

Double rib

This is produced by knitting two stitches and then purling two stitches alternately across the row. Other ribs are formed by choosing any other combination of knit and purl stitches, for example, K3, P1; K5, P3, etc. In every case the knit stitches of the previous row are purled and the purl stitches are knitted.

Invisible cast on for single ribbing

Although ribbing can be cast on in the usual way, you can produce a superior rounded edge with this 'invisible' method, which is firm and elastic, and also forms a casing that can be threaded with elastic, drawstring cording, or a ribbon tie. However, if you

18 Ribbing

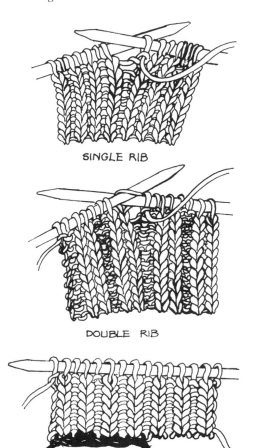

SINGLE RIB

DOUBLE RIB

INVISIBLE CAST ON
FOR SINGLE RIB

are a beginner wait until you have completely mastered the basic stitches first.

Using the single loop method, a length of contrasting yarn and needles two sizes finer than required for ribbing, cast on half the number of sts required plus one. (For abbreviations used, see page 10.)

Proceed with main working yarn as follows:

Row 1 (K1, yf) rep to last st, K1.
Rows 2 & 4 (K1, yf, slP, yb) rep to last st, K1.
Rows 3 & 5 (yf, slP, yb, K1, yf) rep to last st, slP.
Change to correct size needles for ribbing.
Continue to work in K1, P1 rib. Unpick contrast cast on row.

SIMPLE INCREASES AND DECREASES

One of the particular characteristics of knitting is that it is possible to construct and shape the fabric at the same time, even to the extent of creating a three-dimensional garment from a single continuous length of yarn without any joins or seams whatsoever—in other words, shaping takes place as the rows are being knitted.

Increasing and decreasing are the principal ways in which shaping is introduced into knitting—either by making two (or more) stitches out of one, or by knitting two stitches together to make one stitch. This can either be done at the ends of a row to make it wider or narrower, or at any intermediate point within the row. Methods of shaping will be dealt with in much greater detail in Section 3. However, the basic stitch techniques are shown here. Look out for other variations in stitch dictionaries to expand your knowledge.

Simple increasing (Inc 1)
This is the most widely used method of increasing.

A horizontal bar is formed on the left hand side of the increased stitch. In order to balance the appearance of this increase when it is worked at both the beginning and end of a row, increase into the first stitch at the beginning of a row, but into second from last stitch at the end of a row.

1 K or P st in usual way, but do not slip it off LH needle.
2 Insert tip of RH needle into back of same st and K or P into same st again as shown, finally letting st drop from LH needle.
  You now have two sts on RH needle.

Invisible increasing between the stitches
The following method is almost invisible in use so is usually used for increases in the middle of a row.

Make one stitch (m1):
1 Using the tip of RH needle, pick up horizontal strand of yarn between st just worked and next st on LH needle.
2 Place on LH needle, twisting to form loop.
3 K or P into back of loop, thereby avoiding a hole, and complete st as usual.

Decorative increasing
The following three methods produce increases over visible holes in the knitting which can be used for decoration as well as shaping. The eyelet holes so formed are a feature of anything from simple buttonholes and picot edges to complicated lacy patterns, (see also page 64). The method chosen varies according to whether the eyelet is to be placed between K or P sts or a combination of both. All methods produce an extra loop to be worked as a normal stitch on following row.

Yarn forward (yf)
This is used to make an increase between two knit stitches. Bring yarn forward between the needles, as if to purl but knit next stitch instead, thus forming extra loop.

Yarn back (yb)
This means take yarn to back of work between needles.

Yarn round needle (yrn)
Used to make an increase between a knitted and a purled stitch. Bring the yarn forward between needles, and over top of right-hand needle and round between needles again, ready to purl the next stitch.

Also used between two purled stitches, when there is no need to bring the yarn forward between the two needles first.

Yarn over needle (yon)
Used to make an increase between a purled and knitted stitch. Take the yarn over the top of the right-hand needle from front to back, ready to knit the next stitch.

Simple decreasing (dec)
These are worked by knitting or purling two stitches together at the beginning or end of a row, or at any point during a row.

1 On K row, insert RH needle through 2nd and then 1st st on LH needle and knit two together to make a decrease (K2tog). This dec slants to the right.
2 On P row, insert needle Pwise through 1st and then 2nd st and purl two together to make a dec (P2tog). This dec slants to the left. (WS facing)

You will also need to know how to make a decrease which slants in the opposite direction, as decreases are often worked in pairs slanting to left and to right, towards or away from each other. There are two ways of achieving this:

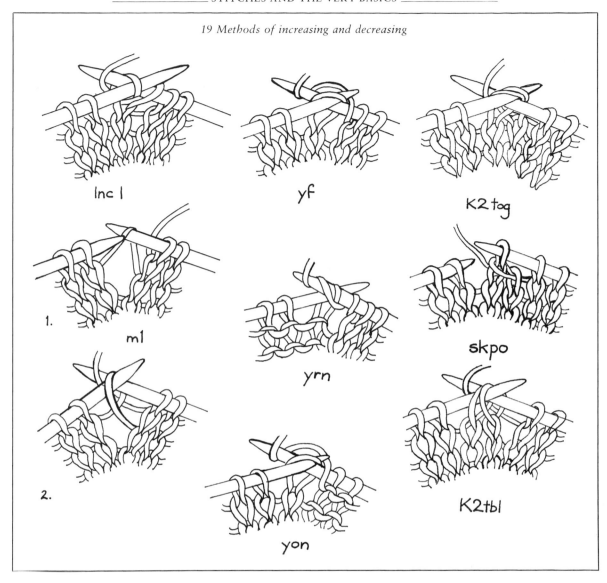

19 Methods of increasing and decreasing

Inc 1

yf

K2 tog

1.

m1

yrn

skpo

2.

yon

K2tbl

(A) Slip stitch decreases

Slip one, knit one, pass slip stitch over (sl1, K1, psso) or skpo.

1 Slip 1st st Kwise on K rows (Pwise on P rows) from LH to RH needle without knitting (purling) it.
2 K (P) next st on LH needle in usual way.
3 Using tip of LH needle, lift slipped stitch over K st (P st) and off RH needle.

This dec slants to the left for knit stitches; right for purl.

Look out for slip, slip, knit (ssk) decs too; these are less well known, but the correct paired dec to K2tog.

1 (Slip 1 Kwise) twice.
2 Insert L needle into front of these sts from left and K2tog.

(B) Knitting two together through back of loops (K2tog, tbl)

Insert tip of RH needle through back of next two sts on LH needle (from L to R on P rows) and knit (or purl) them together. This dec slants to the left for knit stitches; right for purl.

Double decreases (reduce 3 sts down to 1 st)
The simplest method is written as follows: sl1, K2tog, psso (sk2po)

Work as for skpo above but K2tog after slipping first st.

CASTING OFF

Used to secure the finished stitches on a completed section of knitting so that the loops cannot unravel when needles are removed. I have included two cast off methods here, but other methods and variations can be used if preferred.

Two needle method—basic
Knit row Work fairly loosely.
1 K first two sts normally.
2 With LH needle lift first st over second st and drop off RH needle, leaving one st on RH needle.
3 K next st and rep steps 2 and 3, linking all loops along to end of row, or until required No. of sts have been cast off.
4 When one st only is left, break off end of yarn and draw through last st, pulling firmly to secure.

Purl row
Worked in exactly the same way, purling instead of knitting each st before casting off.

Ribbing
Work as before but K or P each st according to rib patt used before casting off sts.

Invisible elastic cast off edge for single ribbing
This looks very professional and is ideal for finishing off neckbands and pocket tops. It is quite tricky to manage, so is only suitable for experienced knitters.

It is necessary to have an odd number of stitches beginning with a K1 on the right side.
1 Work in single rib until 2 rows short of edge.
   Next 2 Rows
   Row 1 K1 (yf, sl 1, yb, K1) repeat to end.
   Row 2 yf, sl 1, (yb, K1, yf, sl 1) repeat to end.
2 Break off yarn, leaving an end about 3 times width of edge to be cast off, and thread into blunt-ended needle.
3 (i) Insert needle in 1st st Pwise and pull yarn through.
   (ii) Insert needle into next P st Kwise, and pull yarn through, leaving both sts on needle.
   First work 2 K sts as foll:

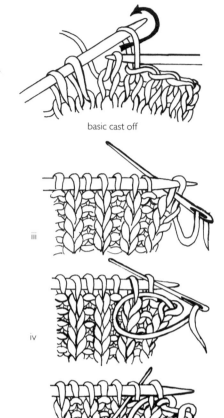

basic cast off

iii

iv

vi

invisible cast off

20 Cast offs

(iii) *Insert needle into 1st st again, Kwise. Pull yarn through and drop st.
(iv) Pass needle in front of next P st and into next K st Pwise, and pull yarn through.
Now work 2 P stitches
(v) Insert needle into 1st P st now on needle, Pwise. Drop st.
(vi) Take needle behind next K st and into back of foll P st, Kwise, and pull yarn through.
(vii) Bring yarn under point of needle, rep from * until sts have been worked. Fasten off.

This completes our basic stitches.

5
Easy textural stitches for big needles

Now that you are familiar with casting on and the two basic knitting stitches, knit and purl, you are ready to attempt all kinds of stitch variations, since all knitting is a permutation of these two fundamental stitches. Many of today's glorious textural yarns have so much surface interest in themselves that complicated stitch patterns can prove superfluous, and may even detract from the full effect of the yarn—hence the frequent use of open textured stitches in knitting patterns designed for fancy textured yarns. Add to this the fact that the easiest way to produce an open texture is to use large needles that allow the work to grow quickly, and you arrive at the perfect combination of factors to enable the inexperienced knitter to produce interesting and creative knitting within a short period of time before boredom or frustration sets in.

Pick up a pair of chunky needles size 6–10 mm (US 10–15) approx and begin with a simple drop stitch, sometimes called elongated stitch.

DROP STITCH

For newer knitters, here is a reminder of what the following abbreviations mean: yf—yarn forward; yrn—yarn round needle.

With RS facing:
Row 1 *Yf, Kl, rep from* to end of row.
Row 2 *Ym, P1, drop extra loop on LH needle, rep from * to end of row.
Row 3 Knit across row, dropping extra loops on LH needle.
Row 4 Purl.
Rep sequence as many times as required.

For a more exaggerated effect you can wind the yarn two or more times round the needle instead of just once, remembering to drop all the surplus loops on the following row.

21 Open textured coat designed and knitted by Sandi Grieve

35

winding yarn around needles

22 Twisted drop stitch

winding yarn around needles

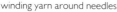

drawing through last loop

It is important to knit at least two firmly knitted rows in perhaps stocking stitch or garter stitch between your drop stitch rows, in order to produce an interesting contrast in stitch size and hold your knitting in shape. This is the whole point of using drop stitch. Otherwise, you might just as well have

23 Detail of multi-textured jacket showing dropstitch and twisted drop stitch (Photo: Raymond Palmer)

knitted the whole thing on larger needles to start with. Alternatively, you could simply change to larger needles for your loose textured rows. But you will have more control over how you want your knitting to develop with the drop stitch method, and you won't have to keep remembering to change needle sizes either.

The currently popular 'Oddpin' needles achieve a similar effect as you knit with one large needle and one small needle on every alternate row.

Drop stitch is probably the most successful yet simple open textured stitch for the relatively inexperienced knitter to use in order to gain maximum effect from fancy textured or brushed yarns. It also looks very effective for open textured summer garments when knitted in tubular knit cotton or man made fibre, ribbon, tape or raffia yarn. (See rag knitted jacket, colour section.)

Or you can use any of the unusual yarn substitutes described at the beginning of the book in order to produce simple yet creative and successful garments that are easy to knit and fast to finish.

An effective variation of drop stitch is the *twisted drop stitch* (sometimes called fancy crossed throw).

With the right side of work facing, insert right needle into stitch as if to knit. Wind yarn first around both needles and then just around right needle in the normal way. Draw through the last loop only, letting the extra loops slip off the needle.

An interesting stitch to follow on from drop stitch

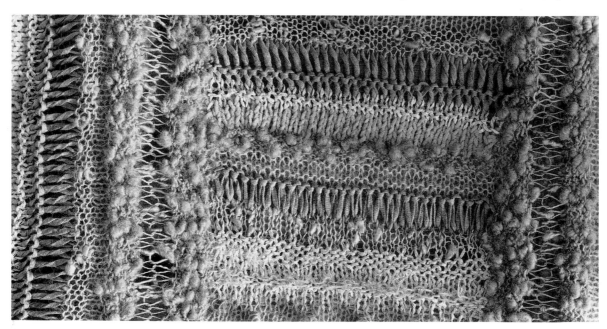

24 (Top) *Wave stitch samples 1 and 2. (Bottom) Wave stitch mistake collar*

is *wave stitch*. This looks very impressive but is not difficult to knit once you understand how the wave sequence is formed. It's all a matter of looking at your knitting as you work and understanding how the stitches produce the desired effect, rather than blindly following instructions without analysing the 'whys and wherefores' of what is happening. A book I can firmly recommend which uses open-textured stitches in a highly creative and un-structured manner is *Creative Knitting, a New Art Form* by Mary Walker Phillips.

Wave stitch 1 (multiple of 10 stitches + 6 extra)
Rows 1 & 2 Knit.
Row 3 (Right side) K6 *yf, K1 (yf and over needle twice) K1, (yf and over needle 3 times) K1, (yf and over needle twice) K1, yf, K6, repeat from * to end.
Row 4 Knit, dropping all extra loops from row 3.
Rows 5 & 6 Knit.

Row 7 K1, repeat from * of Row 3, end last repeat K1 instead of K6.
Row 8 Repeat row 4.
Repeat rows 1–8.

Wave stitch 2 (multiple of 10 stitches + 1 extra)
Rows 1 & 2 Knit.
Row 3 (RS) *(K1, yf) 5 times, K5, rep from * to last st, K1.
Row 4 P1, *P5 (drop yf loop, yrn, P1) 5 times, rep from * to end.
Row 5 *K5 dropping yrn loops, K5, rep from * to last st K1.
Rows 6–8 Knit.
Now rep wave patt but in reverse order, i.e.,
Row 9 *K5 (K1, yf) 5 times, rep from * to last st, K1.
Row 10 P1, (drop yf loop, yrn, P1) 5 times, P5, rep from * to end.
Row 11 *K5, then K next 5 sts, dropping yarn

37

loops, rep from * to last st, K1.
Row 12 Knit.
Rep rows 1–12.

When you have knitted both variations of the wave stitch, look at your samples and see if you can analyse exactly how the wave pattern has been produced in each case.

Basically, the wave is formed by knitting groups of alternating loose and tight stitches, interspersed with ridges of garter stitch which the preceding rows form into wavy bands picked out in relief—hence the name.

Study both samples carefully, and when you have grasped how they both work, you may be able to think of further stitch variations of the same principle to try out for yourself. If so, you can congratulate yourself, as you will have taken the first major step towards becoming a truly progressive knitter.

TURNING MISTAKES TO YOUR OWN ADVANTAGE

You may find you have made the very common mistake of forgetting to alternate your groups of stitches, so that two groups of loose stitches have ended up sitting on top of each other in the same section of the row rather than the sequence alternating correctly. Don't pull the knitting off the needles in frustration—think how you can turn your mistake to advantage instead.

Note how your mistake has distorted the shape of the knitting so that it flares out at either (or both) sides. Without realizing it, you have stumbled upon a novel way of shaping your knitting. How might you use this shaping method to form a useful part of a knitted garment design? How about a wavy collar, fluted cuff or a flared peplum at the bottom of a waisted jacket or cardigan?

Just cast on the number of stitches required for the wave stitch sequence 1 or 2, and keep knitting out of sequence, remembering to repeat your mistake, intentionally this time, until your knitted strip is long enough for the shorter edge to fit around the neckline, lower sleeve edge or waistline of your intended garment. This could be a useful way of livening up a rather plain garment you already own, as the finished edging will drape softly when attached to your completed garment and give it a focal point of interest, especially if you have taken care to choose a yarn which tones or co-ordinates well with the original garment colour.

Pattern Project 3 ✕

Short-sleeved summer top in wave stitch

See colour section
Measurements
To fit sizes 81–91 (97–102) cm/32–36 (38–40)" bust.
Finished chest measurement 107 (117) cm/42 (46)".
Finished length 51 or 61 cm.
Sleeve length from CB neck 43 (45½) cm 17 (18)".
(Figs in brackets refer to larger size)

Materials
450 (550) g total finished weight approx of asstd plain/space dyed cotton and optional thick weight cotton ⑤ ribbon ★★
600 (700) g total finished weight approx for longer version
1 pair size 5½ mm (US 9) needles & set of 4 double-pointed needles size 5½ mm (US 9)

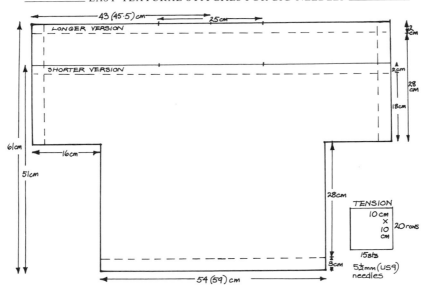

25 Short-sleeved summer top in wave stitch—measurement diagram

Tension

15 sts and 20 rows to 10 cm (4″) over patt.

Abbreviations See page 10.

WAVE PATTERN

Multiple of 20 sts + 1.
Row 1 (RS) * (K1, yf) 10 times, K10, rep from * to last st, K1.
Row 2 P1, *P10 (drop yf loop, yrn, P1) 10 times, rep from * to end.
Row 3 *K10, dropping extra loops, K10, rep from * to last st, K1.
Rows 4–6 Work 3 rows in g st.
Row 7 *K10, (K1, yf) 10 times, rep from * to last st, K1.
Row 8 P1, *(drop yf loop, yrn, P1) 10 times, P10, rep from * to end.
Row 9 *K10, then K10 dropping extra loops, rep from * to last st, K1.
Row 10–12 Work 3 rows in g st.
Rep these 12 rows.

BACK

Choose 1 col for border and cast on 81 (89) sts and work 5 rows g st. Change colour.
Next row K0(4), rep from * in row 1 of wave patt ending K1 (5) and cont in patt as set for 28 cm (11″) approx, ending row 9 of patt, keeping extra sts in st st at sides on larger size, and changing yarn cols

before and after each band of g st. (You may prefer to work g st bands entirely in 1 col throughout)

Sleeve shaping

Cast on 24 sts at beg of next 2 rows, 129 (137) sts and cont in wave patt as set for 18 cm (7″), keeping first and last 4 (8) sts in st st for neater edges. (If a deeper armhole and longer length is preferred, cont for up to 28 cm (11″), holding work up against body periodically to check length, ending with row 3 or 9 of patt.) With border col, work 4 rows of g st.
   Cast off loosely.

FRONT

Work as for back.

MAKING UP

Join shoulders, side seams and underarms, leaving 25 cm (10″) opening for neck.

Sleeve border

With WS facing and set of four 5½ mm needles, using border col, pick up and K15 sts per 10 cm (4″) around sleeve opening—e.g. 60 sts for shorter version or 90 sts for longer version.
   Work 7 rows in g st. Cast off loosely.
   Fold back border onto RS and catch down to edge of wave pattern, enclosing all coloured yarn ends neatly.

Pattern Project 4

Long multi-textured jacket

See colour section

Measurements

One size to fit up to size 102 cm/40″ bust.
Length when completed 74 cm/29″.
Sleeve length from centre back neck 66 cm/26″
including allowance for fullness.

Materials (For this patt, yarn length per ball is given
where possible, to help identify yarn type required)

■ 2 × 50 g balls Col A Nevada Festival shade
6886 (each approx 130 m/142 yd).

☆☆ 2 × 50 g balls Col B Filatura di Crosa Mohair
Multi shade 145 (each approx 160 m/174 yd).

∅ 7 × 50 g balls Col C Robin Mardi Gras shade
5861.

∅∅ 1 × 100 g ball Col D Rowan Cotton Chenille
shade 357 (each approx 140 m/153 yd).

★ 2 × 50 g balls Col E Welcomme Tivoli shade
06 (each approx 67 m/75 yd).

★★ 4 × 50 g balls Col F Jaeger Winter Ribbon
shade 46.

675 g approx total finished weight of jacket.
1 pair of needles size 3¾ mm (US 5) and 1 pair
5 mm (US 8) needles, a 5 mm circular needle—
minimum length 80 cm, and several stitch
holders or spare needles.

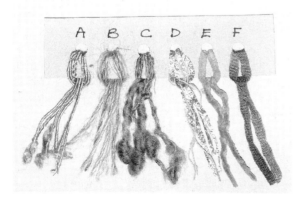

26 Yarn samples used for multi-textured jacket

Tension

16 sts and 22 rows to 10 cm (4″) over patt using size 5
mm needles. Work a test swatch on 32 sts starting
from row 1 of fancy textured stripe patt. If stitch
tension is reasonably accurate, swatch may be used
later in centre panel. Change needle size up or down
1 or more sizes if necessary. Complete patt rep
measures 30 cm (12″) approx, but row tension is
variable and can easily be adjusted during making.

Abbreviations

See page 10. s1P—slip 1 purlwise.

Fancy textured stripe pattern

Row 1–4 With A, work 4 rows rev st st (Purl RS
rows, Knit WS rows).

Row 5–9 With B, work 5 rows st st.

Row 10 With C, *K1, s1P rep from* to end of row.

Row 11–14 With C, work 4 rows rev st st.

Drop stitch

Row 15 With A, *yf, K1, rep from * to end of row.

Row 16 With A, *yrn, P1, drop extra loop, rep from
* to end of row.

Row 17 With C, purl, dropping all extra loops.

Row 18–20 With C, work 3 rows rev st st.

Row 21 With B & C, *K3B, P5C, rep from * to end
of row.

Row 22 With B & C, *P1B, K3C, P4B, rep from * to
end of row.

Row 23 With B & C, *K5B, P1C, K2B, rep from * to
end of row.

Row 24 With B, purl.

Row 25 With B, knit.

Row 26 With B & A, *P5B, make 5 stitch rev st st
bobble in A into next st, (see page 46) P2, rep from *
to end of row.

Row 27 With B, knit.

Row 28 With B, purl.

Row 29 With B & E, *K1B, K1E, rep from * to end
of row.

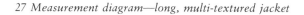

27 Measurement diagram—long, multi-textured jacket

Row 30 With B & E, *P1E, P1B, rep from * to end of row.

Row 31–32 With E, knit 2 rows.

Row 33 With B, *s1P, P1, rep from * to end of row.

Row 34 With B, *K1, s1P, rep from * to end of row.

Row 35 With E, knit.

Row 36 With E, purl.

Row 37–40 With E, work 4 rows rev st st.

Row 41 With A, *K1, s1P, rep from * to end of row.

Row 42–44 With A, work 3 rows st st.

Row 45 With A & F, *K1A, K1F, rep from * to end of row.

Row 46 With F, *yrn, P1, rep from * to end of row.

Row 47 With F, purl, dropping all extra loops.

Row 48–51 With B, purl 4 rows.

Row 52–54 With B, work 3 rows rev st st.

Row 55 With C & D, *K1C, K1D, rep from * to end of row.

Row 56–58 With D, work 3 rows st st.

Row 59 With D & E, *K1D, K1E, rep from * to end of row.

Row 60–62 With E, purl 3 rows.

Row 63 With F, work 1 row in twisted drop st (see page 36).

Row 64 With F, knit.

Row 65 With F, *yf, K one twisted drop st, rep from * to end of row.

Row 66 With A, purl, dropping all extra loops. These 66 rows form textured patt rep. Cont in patt throughout.

Right sleeve and side panels

Beg at cuff, cast on 36 sts in C with size $3\frac{3}{4}$ mm (US 5) needles.

Work in K2, P2 rib for $7\frac{1}{2}$ cm (3″).

Inc row With A, inc in every st (72 sts)

Change to size 5 mm needles and work in patt as shown, starting at row 43 and working straight for 24 cm ($9\frac{1}{2}$″).

Then inc 1 st at each end of RS rows 8 times in all, keeping patt correct (88 sts).

Change to size 5 mm (US 8) circular needle.*

Cast on 56 sts at beg of next 2 rows (200 sts) and work straight for 20 cm (8″).**

Cast off 98 sts loosely at beg of next WS row and transfer rem 102 sts onto spare needle or stitch holders.

Left sleeve and side panels

Work as for R sleeve and side panel to **.

Cast off 98 sts at beg of corresponding RS row and transfer rem sts as before.

Centre back panel

Cast on 32 sts with size 5 mm (US 8) needles and work straight in fancy textured stripe patt, starting at row 1, until length matches that of cast off stitches on side panels, that is, 62 cm ($24\frac{1}{2}$″) approx. Transfer sts to stitch holder.

TO MAKE UP

Join centre panel section to cast off edges of side sections, laying pieces out flat, RS up.

Pin sections together edge to edge, and stitch carefully together with ladder stitch, (see page 152).

Join side and sleeve seams.

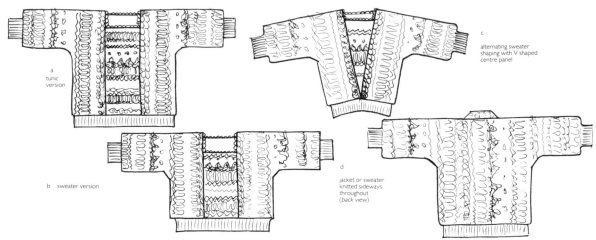

28 Multi-textured jacket variations

Lower welt

With C and size $3\frac{3}{4}$ mm (US 5) needles, RS facing, pick up 162 sts around hem and work in K2, P2 rib for 7.5 cm (3″).

Cast off loosely.

Front and neck band

With C and size 5 mm (US 8) circular needle, RS facing, pick up 14 sts from R front edge of lower welt; 102 sts from R front edge (on holders); 32 sts across back neck (on holder); 102 sts down L front edge (on holders); and 14 sts from L front edge of lower welt (264 sts).

Work in rev st st for 10 cm (4″).

Cast off loosely.

Fold edging in half to WS, and catch down.

SUGGESTED VARIATIONS

(a) Tunic version

Work R and L sleeve and side panels to ** as before.

Work 3 rows rev st st.

Cast off all sts.

Work a second centre panel approx 10 cm (4″) shorter than CB panel.

End both centre panels with 3 rows rev st st and cast off.

Insert between long front edges of side panels.

Add lower welt as before, picking up 192 sts around hem.

(b) Sweater version

As for tunic, but shorter in length.

Work to *, casting on fewer sts, e.g. 40.

(c) Alternative sweater shape with 'V' shaped centre panels

Make 2 v-shaped centre panels by casting on 1 st and inc gradually to 32 sts at neck level.

Ribbed welt may also be shaped if required.

(d) Sideways knitted jacket

Omit centre panels completely.

Work to ** on R sleeve and side panel.

Cast off 102 sts for front.

Cont working across back on rem 98 sts only for 20 cm (8″).

Cast on 102 sts at neck edge.

Work straight for 20 cm (8″).

Cast off 56 sts at beg of next 2 rows (88 sts).

Dec 1 st at each end of RS rows, 8 times in all (72 sts).

Work straight for 24 cm ($9\frac{1}{2}$″).

Dec row (RS facing) K2tog across row (36 sts).

Work in K2, P2 rib for $7\frac{1}{2}$ cm (3″).

Cast off loosely.

You may also like to experiment with your own combination of textured and coloured yarns, using this pattern as a basis for shaping only. Work a test sample; then use this to calculate the number of stitches and rows needed to produce the measurements stated on diagram. The calculations are not complicated as very little shaping is involved, other than basic rectangles, and the number of rows needed can be largely worked out as you go along. Simply keep on knitting until you reach the measurements required.

6
Surface texture

Three-dimensional surface texture may be added to your knitting in a number of different ways to give maximum impact, either by using fashion yarns that are highly textured or with stitch techniques.

FASHION YARNS FOR TEXTURE

This is the simplest option. Choose a fancy textured yarn and just start knitting. The various yarn irregularities, such as 'knops', slubs and tufts will be incorporated randomly into the knitted fabric and will tend to lie on the surface of the knitting, resulting in a highly textured fabric. However, the actual positioning of the lumps and bumps cannot be controlled, and apparently random irregularities are sometimes spaced so regularly that they pop up at almost exactly the same point on each row if you are unlucky. This looks very odd when it isn't intentional—of course it would never happen if you decided to plan it that way!

You will also quickly discover that stocking stitch does not show up fancy textured yarns to advantage since all the interesting 'knobbly bits' unerringly place themselves on the wrong side of the work. This is because yarn is held at the back of the work on knit rows so that any bumpiness of yarn texture causes a natural obstruction which resists being pulled through to the right side with the new knit stitch loops. This partly explains the popularity of reverse stocking stitch patterns in recent years, since the 'wrong' side of the work in this case becomes the right side, and is used as such to advantage.

If you have already experimented with fancy textured yarns, using simple stitches in this way, you'll soon be wanting to take a rather more active role technically in the planning of surface texture within your knitting. Effects such as ridges, ruching, bobbles and cables are created by building up concentrations of extra stitches in one place, at regular or random intervals along the rows of knitting. These 'bunched up' extra stitches cannot lie flat so they spread out above the surface, while still forming an integral part of the knitted fabric. Alternatively, you can add some of these same effects separately at a later stage.

Textured knitting has an obvious tactile appeal so when you first wear your latest knitted creation embellished with bobbles and flaps, don't be surprised to find that you're suddenly the focus of attention for everyone from fascinated small children with sticky fingers to admiring men! For this reason, be careful about where you position any eyecatching three-dimensional features. When standing in a bus queue once, wearing a sweater covered in knitted bell shapes, I turned around to find a wide eyed small boy with one finger stuffed firmly into one of my bells. So be warned . . .

RIDGES

Ridges can be built up across the whole width of your knitting, or in small isolated areas only, in which case they form regular or random tucks on the surface. The depth of ridge can be varied according to individual requirements, but five rows is probably the minimum workable depth to show up sufficiently. It is easier to work your first ridge in a contrasting colour so you can see what you are doing more easily, but once you've grasped the technique it is also very effective to use one colour throughout, which produces a more subtle look using light and shade to maximum effect.

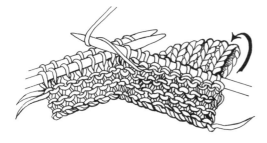

29 Ridges

30 Smocked ridges

1 Work in st st to position of intended ridge, ending with a P row.
2 Change to another col and work a st st stripe at least 5 rows deep ending with a K row.
3 With WS facing, and using a small spare needle, start at the LH edge and pick up first row of loops in new col.
4 Fold col stripe in half towards WS, so that both needles are lying next to each other.
5 Purl together one st from each needle, working across to end of row.
6 Change back to first col and continue in st st until another ridge is required.

An attractive decorative edge can also be incorporated on ridges by working a picot hem turning row (see page 111). You can work ridges very close together so that they overlap, or space them out, with regular or random intervals between each ridge. If you prefer, you can make ridges simply by stitching tucks into the knitted fabric afterwards with a needle and thread, although these will be less elastic than knitted ridges. This is also a useful way of shortening a piece of knitting.

It is extremely effective to pinch ridges together to give a smocked effect, using a needle threaded with contrasting yarn. This effect can be further emphasized by attaching a bead or bow at this point as an additional eyecatching feature.

Try out both a regular and random smocked effect as shown to see which you like best. Then design something simple like a cushion or bag incorporating various ridged effects, before progressing to a simple rectangular sweater shape or sleeveless jacket if you'd like something which you can wear yourself to display your talents.

BOBBLES

Bobbles are rather time-consuming to knit, but fun to make in small doses and very striking. You can place them wherever you like—singly, at random, or in regular fixed patterns on the surface. They can be knitted as you go along (which is neater) or worked separately and attached later, in which case it is effective to use a contrasting colour.

The basic principle never varies—increases are worked into the stitch where the bobble is required and several rows are worked to and fro on these stitches, which are then decreased back down to the original stitch and joined into the background fabric again, either in the same row or several rows later.

You can easily vary the bobble size and texture yourself by increasing the number of stitches worked from three to five or even more, working in stocking stitch or reverse stocking stitch for a crunchier look.

44

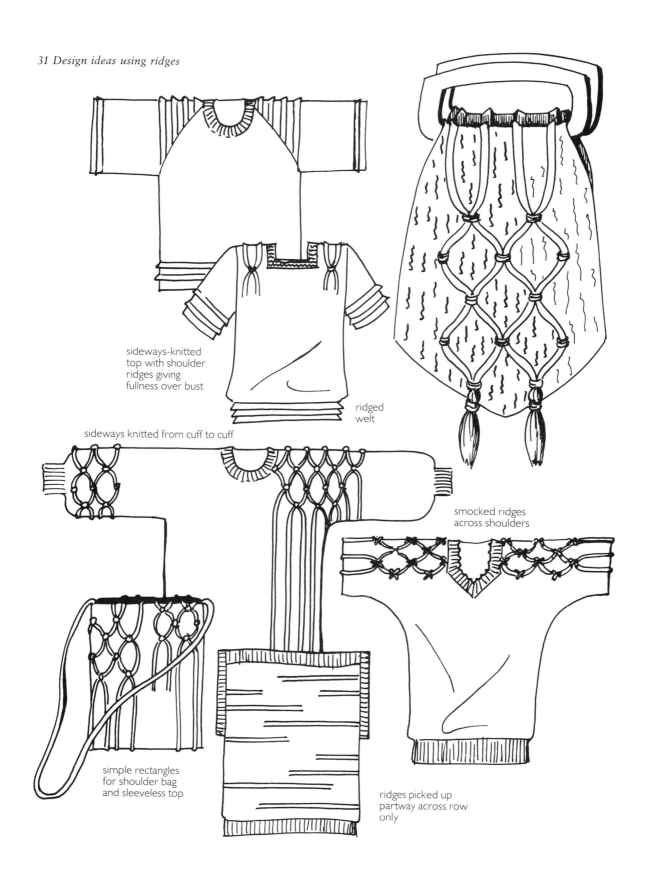

sideways-knitted
top with shoulder
ridges giving
fullness over bust

ridged
welt

sideways knitted from cuff to cuff

smocked ridges
across shoulders

simple rectangles
for shoulder bag
and sleeveless top

ridges picked up
partway across row
only

FIVE STITCH REVERSE STOCKING STITCH BOBBLE

1 K to position of bobble.
2 Make 5 sts out of next st on LH needle as foll: (K1, P1, K1, P1, K1) all into next st. Turn.
3 K5, turn.
4 P5, turn.
5 Rep steps 3 & 4.
6 Using point of LH needle, lift 2nd, 3rd, 4th and 5th st in turn over 1st st and off needle.

32 Flaps

7 K to next bobble position and rep steps 2–6.

For individually made bobbles, cast on 1 st. Work as shown for knitted in bobbles. Break off yarn and slip through last st. Sew in position and fasten off firmly, darning in loose ends.

FLAPS

Like bobbles, flaps can either be knitted in or sewn on afterwards, but to start with you must make them separately. It is necessary to use a stitch which won't curl up, such as garter or moss stitch, unless you make double sided flaps, which have to be stitched together around the edges first.

As it is sometimes difficult to position the flaps satisfactorily while knitting, it is much easier to sew them in place after the background fabric has been completed. However, as with bobbles, you will produce a more professional looking piece of work if you are able to knit the completed flaps in as you go along.

1 Make the required number of flaps in whatever size, colour and shape you want, for example, squares, rectangles, triangles, diamonds. Do not cast off your last WS row, but slip stitches onto a stitch holder and break off yarn.
2 Use a separate stitch holder or safety pin for each flap if possible so you can try out different arrangements of flaps, pinning them roughly in position on a piece of paper or something of similar size to whatever you are planning to make. If it is going to be something wearable, try on one of your existing sweaters and pin your flaps to that to get an idea of how they will look.
3 Knit the background up to the level of the first flap position ending on a knit row.
4 With RS of flap and knitting facing you, place stitchholder with flap in position in front of LH needle and knit together one stitch from each needle until you have worked all flap edge stitches together with background knitting.
5 Continue knitting background fabric until next flap position is reached. Repeat as before.
6 Darn in yarn endings of flaps.

CABLES

Cable patterns are very popular with knitters. They look impressive, yet most patterns are surprisingly easy to knit and can be used for anything from simple panels down the centre of a basic plain knitted garment to spectacular allover designs. They are based on a method of crossing over groups of stitches within a row to give a twisted, rope-like effect, using a third, double-pointed short cable needle which carries the stitches temporarily. If you cannot match the needle size exactly, use the nearest size down to avoid stretching the cable stitches.

Cable patterns usually look best against a background of reverse stocking stitch, which throws them into sharp relief and emphasizes the various twist patterns. The twisting action pulls the work in widthways, so if small areas of cabling are to be introduced in the middle of a plain knitted background it may be necessary to increase the number of stitches used at that point to avoid distortion of the fabric, remembering to decrease again once the cabled area has been completed.

Cable twist from right to left
Worked over 6 sts on a purl background, cable crossed every 6th row.

Pattern repeats over 6 rows and 10 sts.

Cast on a multiple of 10 sts.

Row 1 (WS) K2, P6, K2.

Row 2 & 4 P2, K6, P2.

Row 3 & 5 As 1st row.

Row 6 P2, sl next 3 sts onto cable needle and leave at front of work, K3, then K3 from cable needle, (called C6F) P2.

Plaited cable
Pattern repeats over 8 rows and 13 sts.

Cast on a multiple of 13 sts.

Row 1 (RS) P2, K9, P2.

Row 2 K2, P9, K2.

Row 3 P2, sl next 3 sts onto cable needle and leave at front of work, K3, then K3 from cable needle (called C6F) K3, P2.

Row 4 As 2nd row.

Row 5 & 6 As 1st & 2nd row.

Row 7 P2, K3, sl next 3 sts onto cable needle and leave at back of work, K3, then K3 from cable needle (called C6B), P2.

Row 8 As 2nd row.

Horseshoe cable
Pattern repeats over 8 rows and 16 sts.

Row 1 (RS) P2, K12, P2.

Row 2 K2, P12, K2.

Row 3 & 4 As 1st & 2nd row.

Row 5 P2, C6B, C6F, P2.

Row 6 K2, P12, K2.

Row 7 & 8 As 1st & 2nd row.

You can easily work cables into your own designs, varying the twist patterns and number of stitches used, and incorporating different stitch patterns between the cables if required.

33 Surface textured knitting designed by Maureen O'Dwyer

34 Ideas using surface texture—batwing shapes with flaps. (Top) knitted in one piece from bottom up or from cuff to cuff. (Bottom) V-shaped yoke and angular design

35 *Surface textured stitch patterns* (top row from left) *cable twist, plaited cable, horseshoe cable;* (bottom row from left) *random cables, ruching samples*

Random cables

The panels can either be carefully pre-planned or allowed to wander randomly over the knitting if you prefer, which is both creative and enjoyable, since you can experiment by twisting cables in any direction to see what will happen. Knit a small sample first and see what effects you can produce. Let yourself go!

I have only shown three basic cable patterns here, but you can find many other variations in any knitting stitch dictionary.

RUCHING

This reminds me of the woven seersucker fabric so often used to make checked tablecloths. But when used in knitting the effect looks much more striking, and the surface texture can be emphasized even more with the use of contrasting coloured yarns. It is also extremely easy to knit—something my students always seem surprised to discover when they try knitting a sample.

Cast on required number of stitches and knit in stocking stitch for several rows.
Next row (Pattern) With RS facing, K2, (M1, K1) repeat to last 2 sts, K2.
Knit about 4 rows garter st or rev st st.
Next row (WS) K2, (K2tog) rep to last 2 sts, K2.
Continue in st st until next band of ruched patterning is required.

Other inc methods such as inc 1 or yf can also be used. For example, yf increases will produce a row of decorative holes under the ruching. In addition, try varying the sequence by increasing or reducing the needle size for the ruched pattern bands, or reverse the stitch sequences completely so that the background is worked in garter stitch or purl and the ruched areas in stocking stitch. Don't forget to try a change of yarn texture and colour too.

These are only a small selection of the many three-dimensional stitch patterns available which you can use as a basis for your own designs. Don't be too ambitious at first, and remember to work a sample first to test out your ideas, work out the tension and see if you like the finished effect.

Pattern Project 5 ✖

Drop-shouldered all-in-one jacket with contrast cable detail

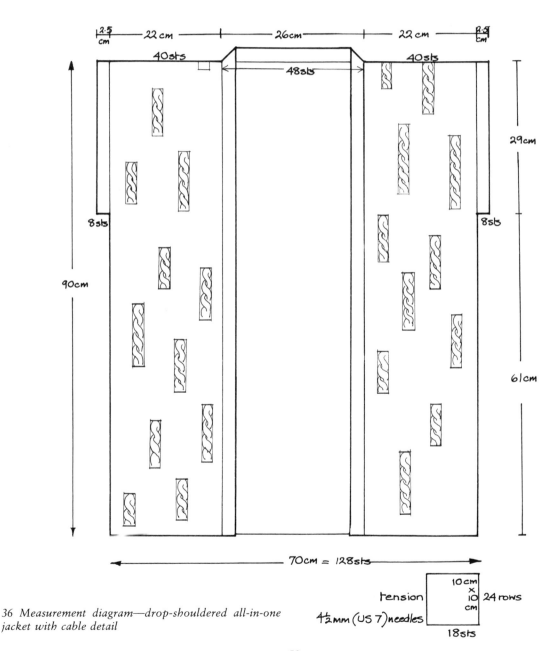

36 Measurement diagram—drop-shouldered all-in-one jacket with cable detail

See colour section

Measurements

One size to fit up to size 102 cm/40″ bust.
Actual measurement across back 70 cm/27½″.
Finished length from CB neck to lower edge
90 cm/35½″.

Materials

Col A—500 g approx fancy cotton ribbon
Col B—100 g approx plain cotton ribbon ★★
Col C—50 g approx plain cotton ribbon
Contrast cols D—250 g approx of assorted col
oddments of cotton ribbon, DK or finer weight
(doubled) cotton or viscose yarns ★★ ② to ⑤
Total finished weight of jacket 900 g approx.
1 pair size 4 mm (us 6) and 4½ mm (us 7) needles (or
circular needles), and 1 cable needle

Tension

18 sts and 24 rows to 10 cm (4″) over st st.

Abbreviations See page 10

C6B—cable 6 back: sl next 3 sts onto cable needle
and leave at back of work, K3, then K3 from cable
needle.
C12B—as C6B, but working 6 sts at a time.

MAIN BODY

Using size 4 mm (us 6) needles & col A, cast on 128
sts at lower edge of back.
Row 1 (slP, K1) to end. Rep this row twice.

Using 4½ mm (us 7) needles, proceed in st st, beg
with K row and work cable twists randomly
throughout jacket using contrasting yarn oddments
as foll:
Row 1 (RS) With A, K to required cable position in
row, K6 col D, with A, K to end.
Row 2 With A, P to cable position, P6D, with A, P
to end.
Row 3 With A, K to cable position, K6D, cont D, K
twice into each of next 6 sts, with A, K to end.
Row 4 With A, P to cable position, P12D, with A, P
to end.
Row 5 With A, K to cable position, K12D, with A,
K to end.

Row 6 As row 4.
Row 7 With A, K to cable position, with D, C12B,
with A, K to end.
Row 8 As row 4.
Rows 9 and 10 As rows 5 and 6.
Rep patt from row 5 at least twice for each cable
block.
Next row (RS) With A, K to cable. With D, K2tog 6
times, with A, K to end.
Next row With A, P across all sts.
Cont straight in st st with cables spaced out as
required (you may have several in varying stages of
progress at once) until work measures 90 cm (35½″).
Divide sts for neck & fronts.
Work 40 sts and slip onto stitch holder, cast off 48
sts for back neck.
Cont on rem 40 sts for 1st front, adding cables
randomly as before until work matches back length
to shoulder, ending with K row.
Next row (WS) Using size 4 mm (us 6) needles, (slP,
K1) to end.
Rep this row twice more.
Cast off. Rejoin yarn to sts on holder and work 2nd
front to match.

Armhole edgings (make 2)

Using size 4½ mm (us 7) needles, cast on 8 sts in col B,
and 2 sts in col C.
Row 1 (WS) K2C, with B, P6, K2.
Rows 2 & 4 With B, P2, K6, P2C.
Rows 3 & 5 As row 1.
Row 6 With B, P2, C6B, P2C.
Rep 6 row cable patt until edging measures 58 cm
(23″), ending with row 3. Cast off.

Neck and front edging band

Proceed as for armhole edgings until band fits all
round neckline and front edges.

MAKING UP

Sew bands in place, with centre of armhole bands to
side edges of jacket at shoulder level, and centre of
neckband to CB neck of body.
Join underarm and edging seams.

51

7

French knitting

Most of us remember french knitting from our childhood days. We spent hours working round and round on a wooden cotton reel with four nails on top, earnestly winding rainbow coloured wool round the nails and hooking off stitches endlessly until we were able to see the end of a tubular knitted cord emerging through the hole. What a sense of achievement we felt and how quiet it kept us!

French knitting is still a valid means of producing knitted cords for adults as well—for functional or decorative knitting projects. But don't bother trying to find a suitable, wooden cotton reel or a knitting nancy either. It is much easier and faster to produce french knitting on two double-pointed knitting needles. I discovered this method in *The Knitters' Almanac*, a marvellous little American book by the unique Elizabeth Zimmermann (published in the

Dover paperback series). She calls it the *idiot cord*, and I am surprised it is not more widely known.

Using 2 double-pointed needles cast on 3 (or 4) stitches.
    *Knit to end of row, but *do not* turn your work.
    Slide the stitches to the other end of the needle.
    Pull yarn firmly and rep from * for desired length.
    To cast off, K1, K2tog, (or K2tog twice), pass 1st st over 2nd.
    Break off yarn and pull loop to secure.

Really keen french knitters can buy a gadget called a *french knitter* (see fig. 10 and page 155 for stockists), which is rather like a mechanized cotton reel with a turning handle. It is absolutely fascinating to use and children adore it, so will happily produce yards of french knitting for you in minutes. This leaves you free to concentrate on the business of incorporating it into your knitting in ever more amazing and ingenious ways.

HOW TO USE IT WHEN YOU'VE MADE IT

The obvious functional uses are as follows: drawstrings, lacing cords, tie bows, shoulder bag straps, connecting mittens together etc. But the creative and decorative possibilities of french knitting open up unlimited extra scope for more exciting textural applications. First make a dozen or more varying lengths of french knitting in assorted colours and yarns.
    Experiment with the following:

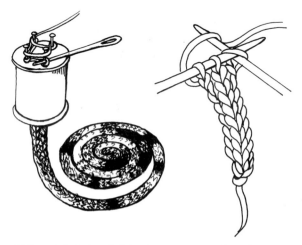

37 French knitting: (left) using a cotton reel; (right) using double-pointed needles

Couching
Arrange plain or striped lengths of french knitting

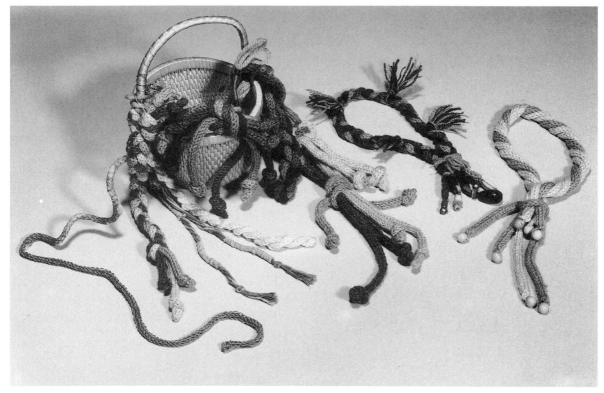

38 *Experimenting with french knitting* (from left) *stuffing and wiring, plaiting, ruching, twisted cord, tied clusters, tasselled plait and twisted cord necklaces*

on the surface of plain knitted garments to make scribble patterns, abstract shapes, initials, names, slogans and logos etc. Couch down firmly with matching or contrasting thread or yarn, either by sewing the underside of the cord firmly down to the background fabric so that the stitches do not show, or by stitching over the cord at regular intervals to make a feature of the stitching.

Outlining
Emphasize particular areas of a garment by outlining in french knitting, for example, on armholes, necklines, shoulders, side seams, and style lines.

Fancy knots
Tie knots at the ends of cords to form a decorative finish and/or attach beads, feathers, sequins, odd earrings, buttons, etc., using the cord yarn ends to attach items firmly, before darning the ends back into the cord itself. You can also knot several cords together to produce interesting shapes and patterns.

Attach to background knitting or use as a fancy edging or hanging border. Marvellous for wall hangings or 'fibre art'.

Tied clusters
Tie several short lengths together in the middle and attach on shoulders (like epaulettes). Short, thick bunches tied together make clusters that can be grouped here and there on a plain knitted background, arranged however you feel looks most effective (See the fitted silk sweater in the colour section.)

Twisted cords
Tie the yarn end(s) of one or more lengths to the door handle, and twist the far end(s) until the whole length is tightly twisted. Keeping the cord under tension, double completely back on itself, and the two lengths of cord will twist naturally round each other like magic along the length. Secure the cord ends together and attach a tassel or bead to add to the finished effect. Make a tassel by folding several

short lengths of yarn in half, then threading looped end through twisted cord and passing cut ends of yarn through loop to secure.

Plaiting

Plait three different coloured cords together, stitching cord ends together firmly. Twisted cords and plaits are ideal for use as tie belts, headbands, straps for shoulder bags, edgings, etc., as well as for outlining knitting features.

Weaving and lacing

Weave french knitting in and out of open textured areas of knitting or make decorative holes (as explained on page 64 and page 68, then slot cording through the holes. If the french knitting is only woven through a few stitches it looks effective to leave the ends dangling, finished with fancy knots, beads, etc.

Knitting

Simply knit lengths of french knitting as if it were yarn, using very large needles (10 mm upwards). The resulting fabric will be strong, very thick in texture, eyecatching and amazingly fast to produce. Try using open textured stitches as well for a different effect.

Stuff it!

Make a tube of french knitting on medium to large needles using very fine yarn such as crochet cotton. Then take a length of thick fluffy yarn, such as a roving (a soft, thick, untwisted rope of yarn fibres), or another contrasting narrower length of french knitting), and thread through the inside of the tube

39 Uses of french knitting (from top) *couching, fancy knot, stuffed tubes*

41 Decorative use of stuffed and ruched French knitting, with added bobbles on plain knitted background

40 Designs using outlining

using a wide-eyed blunt-ended needle. The contrasting yarn inside will be seen clearly through the open textured french knitting stitches.

Wiring
Thread pipe cleaners or flexible wiring through the french knitting so that it can be twisted and bent into fixed rigid shapes. Fine or thick wire can be used according to the degree of delicacy or strength required, but remember the result is unlikely to be washable so is only suitable for decorative use.

Ruching
Once again, stuff the tube, but this time make sure the stuffing is strong and unlikely to break. Fix a length of strong thread or yarn to one end of the french knitting, threading it through as before and out the far end. Draw threaded yarn up tightly so that the knitting gathers up, either along its entire length or just here and there. (This process can also be used effectively for any of the tubular knitting

yarns now on the market.) Couch down on a knitted background, or use in any of the ways previously mentioned.

Giant sized knitting
Last but not least—back to simple childhood pleasures. If you know a child who wants something a little more ambitious than ordinary french knitting, but who isn't yet up to handling knitting needles, try giant size french knitting for a change. Tape used matchsticks around the outside of an empty toilet roll tube, and work the yarn round and round in the traditional way. Many more stitches than the traditional four as used for the cotton reel method are possible, and will produce a much larger knitted tube suitable for doll's clothes etc.

8

Adding embellishments, buttons and trimmings

In addition to adding knitted surface decoration, you can also draw on a vast range of embellishments which are *not* knitted. You may not previously have associated some of them with knitting at all, but they can transform a plain piece of knitting into something really special. This decorative kind of knitwear is always expensive to buy, so by knitting it yourself you will have something special yet affordable. The end result will never look 'run of the mill', and is bound to attract comments and compliments, especially if you are able to say that you made it yourself.

Non-knitted embellishments can either be incorporated into your knitting as you go along, or added after completion of the background fabric so you can try out and rearrange the finished effect before committing yourself. You can also decorate any existing plain knitted items that need livening up. However, incorporating embellishments as you go along is undoubtedly neater, and will also be quicker as long as you don't mind planning your work in advance.

BEADS AND SEQUINS

There are many types of beads and sequins available; they can be knitted in so closely together on your knitting that they cover the entire surface or be scattered widely apart to form a regular or random pattern. If you are using a fairly large quantity it makes sense to knit them in as you go along, but the hole must be big enough to take the yarn, and on sequins it must be placed near the edge and not in the middle or it will not lie flat against the knitting. Beads must not be too heavy or they will weigh the work down.

42 *Bead and sequin knitting*

56

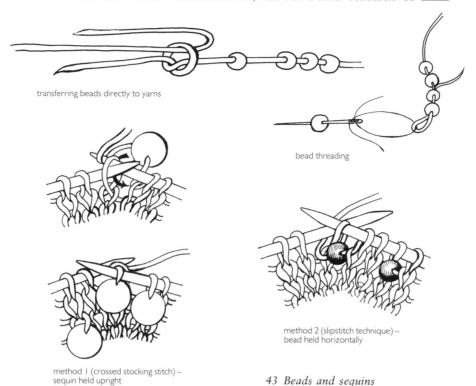

transferring beads directly to yarns

bead threading

method 1 (crossed stocking stitch) –
sequin held upright

method 2 (slipstitch technique) –
bead held horizontally

43 Beads and sequins

Threading onto yarn

If you plan to use the same beads or sequins throughout and you bought them pre-strung, you may be able to transfer them straight onto the knitting yarn without any individual threading. Knot the bead string and knitting yarn together as shown, and with luck you will be able to slide the beads over the knot onto the yarn ready for use. Simple!

Loose beads must be threaded individually. If you cannot thread the beads or sequins directly onto the yarn because the yarn is too thick to pass through the eye of a fine enough needle, use this method:
1 Thread about 25 cm (10″) of sewing thread through a 15 cm (6″) loop of knitting yarn as shown, then thread both ends of thread through a fine sewing needle.
2 Thread the beads or sequins onto the needle and slide them down the thread onto the yarn, always leaving one bead on the yarn loop to hold it in position.

Forward planning

You need to estimate the number and order of beads to be used in advance for each ball of yarn, because once they have been threaded their order and number cannot be changed. Plan the order particularly carefully if you are using a definite pattern sequence, arranging the beads in rows on some corrugated cardboard to keep them temporarily in position. It is impossible to estimate exactly how many beads will be needed per ball of yarn, so divide the number of beads required by the approximate number of balls to be used overall, threading a few more onto the first ball of yarn than your calculations suggest in order to be absolutely safe.

Knitting in beads and sequins

Beads and sequins are usually incorporated onto a stocking stitch background, but they also look extremely effective against openwork lace patterns as the beads can be arranged to hang in the open spaces rather than lying flat against the background fabric. They are usually knitted in on RS rows unless very dense beading is required. Keep the tension on bead stitches as tight as possible.

Method 1 (crossed stocking stitch)
This method is appropriate for objects with holes

close to the edge, droplet beads and pendant shapes, and was used in the eighteenth and nineteenth centuries for intricate purse knitting. The yarn strand holding the object is almost upright in position, so allowing the object to hang correctly.

1 With RS facing, work to position for first bead. Push bead (or sequin) up to stitch close to back of work.
2 Knit next stitch through back of loop, pushing bead through loop to front of work at the same time. Knit to position of next bead.

Method 2 (slipstitch technique)
This is only suitable for designs with at least one stitch between each bead. The bead lies on the front of the work, held in position by a horizontal strand. It is simpler to knit than the first method.

1 With RS facing knit to position for first bead. Bring yarn forward and push bead close to previous stitch at front of work.
2 Slip next stitch Kwise, take yarn back and K to position of next bead.

JEWELLERY, BUTTONS, SHELLS, SEEDS, SMALL TOYS

Anything which has a hole in it, or can be pierced to make a hole can be added in the same way as beads and sequins. The possibilities are endless—odd earrings, junk rings, pendants and brooches, plastic cracker toys, novelty rubbers, etc. are all suitable. Cut out geometric shapes from scraps of leather, fabric and felt, and punch or pierce a hole in one corner. Try hearts, diamonds, circles and crescents or whatever other shapes you like—just make sure you can wash or dry clean them first.

A fine drill will be needed for hard objects like nuts and shells, but other items can be pierced with the point of a needle. If you want to melt a hole in plastic objects, heat the needle in a flame first, holding it with a pair of pliers so you don't burn your fingers.

SEQUIN STRIP

This is the perforated strip left over from making sequins. It comes in rolls and is available from handicraft suppliers. Cut into small pieces or use as an unusual edging in small areas of a garment. You will need to crochet along an edge row of holes first before you can start knitting, or you may prefer to thread yarn loops through each hole so you can attach a foundation row onto your knitting needle. Alternatively, just stitch or tie on a segment of the strip to the completed fabric.

FEATHERS

You can easily plait or bind feathers into yarns, and although they are very expensive to buy it is also possible nowadays to buy feathered yarns from certain spinners. Either way, you only need small quantities, or else you will end up looking like a trussed chicken! Feathers are most suitable for

44 Jewellery and other objects incorporated into knitting

edgings such as necklines, and are best woven into the knitting, or used as accessories, since they are not really suitable for knitting in.

PIPE CLEANERS

Use the fluffy coloured pipe cleaners now available, not the short plain white ones. They are suitable for knitting a few stitches at a time or can be woven into your knitting. They are also a useful way of adding rigidity and can be bent into the shape you require, so are very appropriate for small objects like toys or hanging mobiles.

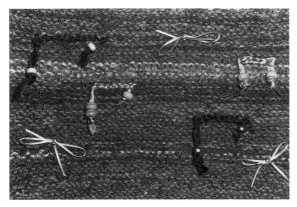

45 Ideas for ribbon decoration on colour blended garter stitch background

RIBBON WEAVING AND BOWS

Ribbons may be added to knitting in a number of decorative ways, and ribbon yarns are now widely available from high street yarn suppliers as well as from the usual haberdashery counters.

● You can transform a plain garment into something very special by tying on bows or streamers.

● Weave ribbon in and out of your knitting, or thread ribbon through cable stitch or similar raised stitches to emphasize particular features.

● Knit short lengths of ribbon into a garment by picking up small groups of stitches from the surface onto a needle and casting off the stitches with ribbon, leaving a few centimetres dangling at each end of the worked stitches. Decorate with knotted-on beads.

Alternatively, ribbon may be knitted in while the work is in progress; knit the ribbon together with the background yarn for the required number of stitches.

46 Ribbon weaving and knitting

EMBROIDERY

Embroidery is an extremely effective way of enriching a knitting design and adding extra texture and colour. A large number of traditional embroidery stitches can be used—for example, cross stitch, blanket stitch, chain stitch, running stitch, stem stitch, feather stitch, couching and french knots. Appliqué and quilting techniques add an extra dimension by building up layers.

The best known embroidery stitch for knitting is called swiss darning or duplicate stitch. This technique is explained in detail in the colour section on page 82 as it is primarily used to add extra colour rather than texture. However, there is no reason why it cannot be used to add textural decoration as well, since the technique covers the required number of stitches completely with a new yarn, so resulting in a double thickness of fabric. Try covering botany wool with fluffy mohair, or cotton with small amounts of silk or linen yarn.

9
More stitch patterns to try

The enormous boom in fancy textured and novelty yarns created a huge demand for simple stitch patterns requiring a bare minimum of knitting technique. These have undoubtedly been responsible for attracting countless new knitters to the craft in recent years, many of whom have now progressed to the point where they are looking for something more advanced to get their teeth into. Here is a further selection of stitch patterns you may like to try, together with some suggestions for their use. The stitches are used in various different ways to produce particular types of texture. Pick out one which appeals to you and knit up a swatch to get the feel of it. If you like it, think how it might look in a different weight, colour or type of yarn. Try to visualize how you might incorporate it into a design of your own, possibly copying or adapting an idea you've seen somewhere else. Even better, think of a completely original way of using the stitch in question.

Several stitch patterns can also be mixed together successfully in the same piece of knitting, in either blocks or panels divided by a narrow line of plain stitches. Do knit swatches first to check that the stitch tensions are compatible with each other. Remember that these are only a tiny selection of the hundreds of stitch patterns available.

SOLID FABRICS

These are made up of knit and purl stitches used in basic sequences. The simple patterns are suitable for even inexperienced knitters to follow. The combination of smooth and ridged stitches produces subtle yet interesting textured effects which are best suited to smooth plain yarns. Basket stitch is one example.

Basket stitch
Pattern repeats over 12 rows.
Cast on a multiple of 6 sts.
Row 1 Knit.
Row 2 Purl.
Row 3 *K1, P4, K1 rep from * to end.
Row 4 *P1, K4, P1 rep from * to end.
Row 5 As row 3.
Row 6 As row 4.
Row 7 Knit.
Row 8 Purl.
Row 9 *P2, K2, P2 rep from * to end.
Row 10 *K2, P2, K2 rep from * to end.
Row 11 As row 9.
Row 12 As row 10.

Stitch charts
Stitch patterns can also be shown in chart form, which is a far briefer and more logical way of presenting pattern instructions than written directions, since the visual format clearly shows the knitter how the pattern has actually been created. This leads to a far greater understanding of the technicalities involved and is more likely to encourage experimentation and creativity. However, for reasons which have never been clear, stitch charts (together with all visual instructions, such as measurement diagrams) went out of use in English knitting patterns for many years, so that a whole generation of knitters, myself included, grew up to be unfamiliar with their use, except for the minority who knitted up translated versions of continental patterns. With the ever increasing popularity of these, it is interesting to see that English and American patterns are reverting to chart usage at last, and not before time. Not only do stitch symbols

47 Stitch pattern selection: (top row from left) basket stitch, pique triangle stitch, welting fantastic; (centre row) zig-zag pattern, horseshoe print, bell motif; (bottom row) embossed leaf pattern, barrel stitch, crossed insertion

in chart form do away with the language barrier (even Japanese patterns can be clearly understood), but they are a great deal easier to follow once you know how, and it only takes a minute or two to learn. Look at the chart for basket stitch and you will see what I mean.

Pique triangle stitch
Pattern repeat over 12 rows.
Cast on multiple of 12 sts
Row 1 *K6, P1, K5 rep from * to end.
Row 2 *P4, K3, P5 rep from * to end.

Row 3 *K4, P5, K3 rep from * to end.
Row 4 *P2, K7, P3 rep from * to end.
Row 5 *K1, P9, K2 rep from * to end.
Row 6 Purl.
Row 7 *P1, K11 rep from * to end.
Row 8 *K1, P9, K2 rep from * to end.
Row 9 *P3, K7, P2 rep from * to end.
Row 10 *K3, P5, K4 rep from * to end.
Row 11 *P5, K3, P4 rep from * to end.
Row 12 Purl.

The chart
1 The chart shows the front of the fabric with each row of the chart being read in the direction the row is knitted—that is, odd numbered right side rows are read from right to left and even numbered wrong side rows are read from left to right.

61

2 Each square on the chart contains a symbol which represents one stitch, and there is always a key to explain every symbol used. Symbols usually resemble the stitch they are representing so that it is easier to recognize and remember them by shape alone.

BASKET STITCH CHART

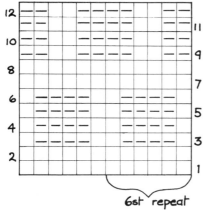

48 Basket stitch chart

3 The main thing to remember is that looking at the chart is like looking at the actual stitches from the right side. So the symbol for stocking stitch, which is usually shown as a blank square ☐ , indicates that you knit when the right side of the work is facing you and purl when the wrong side is facing you. The symbol for reverse stocking stitch, shown here as ⊟ means that you purl on the right side and knit on the wrong side. This may sound confusing, but works very well in practise. Instructions for all other stitches are explained on whichever side of the knitting is facing you at the point where the symbol is shown.

4 The pattern repeat is given below the stitch chart, which means that you continue to repeat the number of stitches shown within the repeat as many times as necessary—usually until the end of the row.
See if you can write a chart for the pique triangle stitch yourself. (The answer is shown on page 64.) The system can also be used for planning or recording your own patterns. (See fig. 91.)

Now that knitting is firmly established in the public mind as not only a popular leisure pastime but also a design centred craft in the artistic sense, there is a growing demand for more technically challenging, yet fashionable patterns. The trend towards finer yarns and more complex stitch techniques is encouraging greater use of stitch symbols and charted patterns. This helps thinking knitters to see for themselves how stitch patterns are actually planned, while learning the various knitting techniques involved.

BIAS FABRICS

Bias knitted fabrics have stitches running diagonally across the width, either to right or left. If these are combined to move in both directions at once they form chevron patterns. These are knitted by increasing and then decreasing stitches across the row, thus forming a waved effect that is particularly effective when knitted in rows of different colours. Even blocks of normal horizontal rows can be made to 'wave' if they are inserted between chevron knitted rows as shown here.

Welting fantastic
Pattern repeats over 12 rows.
Cast on a multiple of 11 sts.
Rows 1–6 Starting with purl, work 6 rows in st st.
Rows 7, 9 & 11 *K2tog, K3, m1, K1, m1, K3, K2tog, rep from * to end.
Rows 8, 10 & 12 Purl.

Try substituting other textured stitches for rows 1–6 above, for example, twisted drop stitch on page 36. You will be amazed how many novel chevron effects you can create.

OPENWORK PATTERNS

Decorative ladders

Back at the beginning of the book you learnt how to turn the disaster of a dropped stitch to your advantage and make an attractive feature out of the resulting ladder. But it's also possible to plan decorative ladder patterns in advance, deciding precisely where, how long, and how wide you want them for a particular effect.

50 *Decorative ladders*

49 *Decorative ladders*

First knit to the position in the row where you require the bottom of the ladder to begin (or rather end, since the finished ladder will unravel back to this spot). This is called the platform. Make a yarn

forward and knit the next two stitches together. Can you see the reasons for this? The yarn forward makes a new stitch with a hole underneath, marking where the ladder will eventually unravel back to and stop, since the new stitch did not exist before this point and can unravel no further. To keep the stitch numbers constant the following two stitches are knitted together. Carry on knitting, making platforms for other ladders as you go.

When you have knitted the intended number of rows for your first ladder, knit to the stitch directly above the hole made by the yarn forward, and drop it so that it unravels, leaving an open ladder space about three times the width of the original stitch. (Incidentally this can be a useful way of enlarging the width of a garment.) Carry on knitting, replacing the dropped stitch by picking up the last bar of the ladder and knitting it before continuing. Drop other ladders where planned. You may leave the ladders open if you wish or decorate in the manner of drawn thread embroidery as shown. You can also plan double width ladders by making a platform of two cast off stitches. On the next row knit up the loops of these two cast off stitches and build the ladder on these, remembering to replace the dropped stitches above the top of the ladder as before.

PIQUE TRIANGLE STITCH

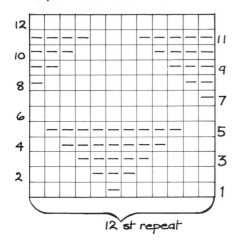

51 Pique triangle chart (see page 62)

ZIG ZAG PATTERN

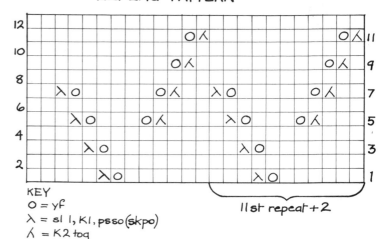

KEY
O = yf
λ = sl 1, K1, psso (skpo)
⋏ = K2 tog

52 Zig-zag pattern chart

LACE

Knitted lace is made by balancing decorative eyelet increases with an equal number of decreases to produce an intricate openwork fabric. The decrease stitches must cancel out the increase stitches exactly for a constant width of fabric, although several rows may sometimes be worked before the balance is corrected entirely. Eyelet patterns differ from lace in that they consist purely of decorative holes worked on a plain background, whereas the formation of lace patterns is more complex and affects the entire fabric. These patterns usually need both stretching and blocking to show the work to best effect.

Zig zag pattern
Pattern repeats over 12 rows.
Cast on a multiple of 11 sts plus 2 extra.
Row 1 K6 *yf, skpo, K9 rep from * ending last rep K5.
Row 2 (and every alternative row) (WS) Purl.
Row 3 K7 *yf, skpo, K9 rep from * ending last rep K4.
Row 5 K3 *K2tog, yf, K3, yf, skpo, K4 rep from * ending K3.
Row 7 *K2, K2tog, yf, K5, yf, skpo rep from * ending K2.
Row 9 K1, *K2tog, yf, K9 rep from * ending K1.
Row 11 *K2tog, yf, K9 rep from * ending K2.

The stitch chart for this pattern is included so you can see how symbols are used for increase and decrease stitches in a chart. It will also enable you to see more clearly how the pattern is formed.

Horseshoe print pattern
One of the most popular classic Shetland lace patterns—effective, yet quite simple to knit. The pattern was originally inspired by the imprint of horseshoes on wet sand.
Pattern repeats over 8 rows.
Cast on a multiple of 10 sts plus 1 extra.
Row 1 (WS) Purl.
Row 2 K1, *yf, K3, sk2po, K3, yf, K1, rep from * to end.
Row 3 Purl.
Row 4 P1, *K1, yf, K2, sk2po, K2, yf, K1, P1 rep from * to end.
Row 5 K1, *P9, K1 rep from * to end.
Row 6 P1, *K2, yf, K1, sk2po, K1, yf, K2, P1 rep from * to end.
Row 7 As row 5.
Row 8 P1, *K3, yf, sk2po, yf, K3, P1 rep from * to end.

EMBOSSED PATTERNS

These consist of raised motifs built up of extra stitches that are 'clustered' into the background fabric in various ways. They are fiddly but are not as difficult to knit as one might expect. *Detached* clusters are loose motifs built up from and attached to the fabric by one stitch only, for example, bobbles. (See pages 44, 45.)

Bell motif

This is one of my favourite stitches, the shape reminding me of cottage garden foxgloves. It is also a particularly attractive example of the type of stitch known as a *semi-detached* cluster—that is, a group of raised stitches cast on between two stitches with the raised shape built in over a number of rows and gradually reduced down to nothing as the motif is completed.

Pattern repeats over 14 rows.

Cast on a multiple of 4 sts plus 4 extra.

Row 1 P4, *cast on 8 sts, P4 rep from * to end.
Row 2 *K4, P8 rep from * to last 4 sts, K4.
Row 3 P4, *K8, P4 rep from * to end.
Row 4 *K4, P8 rep from * to end K4.
Row 5 P4, *skpo, K4, K2tog, P4 rep from * to end.
Row 6 *K4, P6, rep from * to last 4 sts, K4.
Row 7 P4, *skpo, K2, K2tog, P4, rep from * to end.
Row 8 *K4, P4 rep from * to last 4 sts, K4.
Row 9 P4, *skpo, K2tog, P4, rep from * to end.
Row 10 *K4, P2, rep from * to last 4 sts, K4.
Row 11 P4, *K2tog, P4, rep from * to end.
Row 12 *K4, P1, rep from * to last 4 sts, K4.
Row 13 P4, *K2tog, P3, rep from * to last st, P1.
Row 14 Knit.

This stitch uses up a great deal of yarn, but the effect is easily worthwhile.

Embossed leaf pattern

This is another favourite of mine and an example of an attached embossed motif—extra stitches are built into the background fabric by increasing, and then decreasing, to produce an embossed 'blister' shape. Instructions can be varied to form circles, ovals, leaves or diamond shapes as required. Look in any stitch dictionary for other similar examples if you like the effect as much as I do. During the nineteenth century, embossed shapes were often used in beautiful white knitted cotton patchwork quilts—I am lucky enough to own an old quilt which originally belonged to my grandmother. But it is good to see that many old knitted quilt patterns have now been revived by Tessa Lorant in her book *Knitted Quilts and Flounces* (see bibliography).

Pattern repeats over 20 rows.

Cast on a multiple of 7 sts plus 6 extra.

Row 1 P6, *yon, K1, yrn, P6 rep from * to end.
Row 2 *K6, P3 rep from * to last 6 sts, K6.
Row 3 P6, *K1, (yf, K1) twice, P6 rep from * to end.
Row 4 *K6, P5 rep from * to last 6 sts, K6.
Row 5 P6, *K2, yf, K1, yf, K2, P6 rep from * to end.
Row 6 *K6, P7 rep from * to last 6 sts, K6.
Row 7 P6, *K3, yf, K1, yf, K3, P6 rep from * to end.
Row 8 *K6, P6 rep from * to last 6 sts, K6.
Row 9 P6, *skpo, K5, K2tog, P6 rep from * to end.
Row 10 *K6, P7, rep from * to last 6 sts, K6.
Row 11 P6, *skpo, K3, K2tog, P6, rep from * to end.
Row 12 *K6, P5 rep from * to last 6 sts, K6.
Row 13 P6 *skpo, K1, K2tog, P6 rep from * to end.
Row 14 *K6, P3, rep from * to last 6 sts, K6.
Row 15 P6, *sk2po, P6 rep from * to end.
Rows 16, 18 & 20 Knit.
Rows 17 & 19 Purl.

Many blister stitch patterns benefit from blocking (see page 151). Moisten the knitting after completion and place a mould such as a button, bead or pebble under each blister; smooth the fabric over the moulds and pin in position until dry to show the blister shape off to full advantage. Non-wearable knitted pieces can also be starched to hold the shape in position even more firmly.

Barrel stitch

Yet another variation of a stitch cluster.

Pattern repeat over 12 rows.

Cast on a multiple of 4 sts plus 4 extra.

Row 1 P4, *cast on 8 sts, P4 rep from * to end.
Row 2 K4, *P8, K4 rep from * to end.
Row 3 P4, *K8, P4 rep from * to end.
Rows 4-9 Repeat rows 2 & 3 three times.
Row 10 K4, *cast off 8 sts, K4 rep from * to end.
Row 11 Purl.
Row 12 Knit.

If you wish to alternate the spacing of succeeding rows of barrels, work 6 knit or purl stitches as appropriate at the beginning of the row, and 2 stitches at end. Barrels may also be varied in width or length by increasing the number of stitches or rows as required.

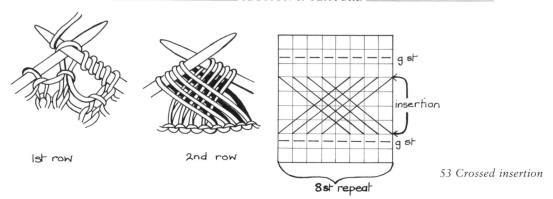

1st row   2nd row

g st

insertion

g st

8 st repeat

53 Crossed insertion

CROSS-OVER MOTIFS AND PATTERNS

Crossed insertion

A decorative open-textured insertion divided by bands of stocking stitch or garter stitch.

Pattern repeats over 2 rows.

Cast on a multiple of 8 sts.

Row 1 *K1, yf and over needle 4 times, rep from * to end.

Row 2 *(Sl 1, drop 4 extra loops.) Rep 7 times so that you have 8 long sts on R needle. Pass L needle through first 4 sts and lift them over second group of 4 sts. Transfer all 8 sts carefully to L needle and knit in this order. Rep from * to end of row.

54 Design ideas using texture

Dividing band

Work several rows st st or garter st, ending with (WS) knit row. The insertion can be varied by increasing or decreasing the number of extra loops in row 1, and also be crossing over different numbers of stitches in row 2.

USING DESIGN TO WORK FOR YOU

Now that you've finished working through the texture section it's a good plan to jot down a few design ideas on paper. Don't worry if you're no good at drawing—as long as *you* know what you mean it really doesn't matter what your rough scribbles look like to anyone else. Just doodle away without thinking too much about it—the simple act of putting pen to paper is usually enough to get the thought processes grinding into action. That undisciplined jumble of possibilities floating around in your head will gradually unscramble itself and you'll find that a definite direction begins to emerge. New stitches spring to mind; one chain of thought leads to another . . . .

A simple ribbed welt to start with, maybe, then a few rows of bobbles? How about some ridges next, or short lengths of ribbon threaded through in the opposite direction? Possibly a block of fancy stitches worked down one side, or would they look better knitted across the width higher up? With any luck you'll soon have a page full of rough sketches in front of you. So many possibilities! So many ways to create interesting textures! Don't worry about shaping problems for now. Stick to basic squares and rectangles for the time being and just enjoy the challenge of starting to design your own knitwear for the very first time, approaching it in whichever way feels right for you personally.

You can use the patterns included in this section to help you with ideas initially. Knit them just as they are adding a few touches of your own too, or simply use the shapes as a framework for your own textures; it's entirely up to you. If you already feel that you've discovered a great deal about texture that you didn't know before, why not start putting it into practise right *now*?

Pattern Project 6 ✕ ✕

Sleeveless jacket with picot edging

See colour section

Measurements

To fit small to med 81–86 cm/32–34″ bust, med to large 91–102 cm/36–40″ bust.

Finished measurements all round at hem 101 (111) cm/39¾ (43¾)″.

Finished jacket length may be shortened or lengthened by omitting or adding bands of colour stitch patterns below armhole level.

Materials

100 g each of cols A & B ⎱ Jumper weight
50 g each of cols C, D & F ⎰ shetland wool ☒ (knits as 4 ply)
50 g of col E — Mohair (optional ☆☆ or shetland ☒

Quantities as stated here have been rounded up to

nearest available units of yarn weight, and include sufficient allowance for individual variations in colour, size and length of jacket required. Knitting kits are also available (see page 155).

Total finished weight of jacket approx 260 g (small to med); 300 g (large).

1 size 2¾ mm (US 2) and 3¼ mm (US 3) circular needles (minimum length 80 cm (31½″).

20 cm (8″) washable terylene wadding (optional).

Tension

26 sts and 32 rows to 10 cm/4″ in st st on size 3¼ mm (US 3) needles.

Abbreviations See page 10.

mb—Make bobble as follows: (K1, P1, K1, P1, K1) into next st. Turn, K5, turn, P5, turn, lift 2nd, 3rd, 4th & 5th sts over 1st st, turn.

MAIN BODY

Col A Cast on 247 (273) sts with size 2¾ mm circular needle.

Work 12 rows st st.

Work picot edge turning row as foll: K1, *K2tog, yf. Rep from * to last 2 sts, K2.

Work 13 rows st st.

Col B Change to size 3¼ mm circular needle. *Work simple eyelet patt thus:* Work 4 rows st st.

Row 5 K2(3), *K2tog, yf, K3, rep from * 49 (54) times to end of row. Work 3 rows st st.

Ridged eyelet patt

Col C K 2 rows.

Row 3 K1, *K2tog, yf, rep from * to last 2 sts, K2. K 2 rows, ending with a RS row.

Horseshoe print patt (multiple of 10 sts + 1)

Col D Row 1 WS (and every foll WS row) P.

Row 2 K4 (2) *yf, K3, sk2po, K3, yf, K1, rep from * to last 3 (1) sts, K3 (1).

Row 4 K3 (1), P1, *K1, yf, K2, sk2po, K2, yf, K1, P1, rep from * to last 3 (1) sts, K3 (1).

Row 6 K3 (1), P1, *K2, yf, K1, sk2po, K1, yf, K2, P1, rep from * to last 3 (1) sts, K3 (1).

Row 8 K3 (1), P1, *K3, yf, sk2po, yf, K3, P1, rep from * to last 3 (1) sts, K3 (1).

Row 9 Purl.

Garter st ridge patt

Col E K 2 rows.

Simple stripe patt

Col F Work 4 rows st st.

Col C Work 2 rows st st.

Col F Work 2 rows st st.

Cat's paw patt (multiple of 12 sts +9)

Col A Work 6 rows st st.

Row 7 K8 (9) *yf, sk2po, yf, K9, rep from * to last 11 (12) sts, yf, sk2po, yf, K8 (9).

Row 8 and every foll WS row, purl.

Row 9 K6 (7) *K2tog, yf, K3, yf, skpo, K5, rep from * to last 1 (2) sts, K1 (2).

Row 11 As row 7.

Rows 12–16 St st.

Border stripe patt

Col F Work 2 rows st st.

For short version of jacket go forward to *** (after cloverleaf patt). Cont for longer version thus:

Vertical stripe patt (strand cols *very loosely* across back of work)

Col D Work 2 rows st st.

Row 3 *K1D, K1C, rep from * to end of row, ending K1D.

Row 4 *P1D, P1C, rep from * to end of row, ending P1D.

Rows 5–8 As rows 3 & 4.

Col D Work 2 rows st st.

Rev st st ridge patt

Col F Work 2 rows st st.

Row 3 (RS.) Purl.

Row 4 Knit. Work 2 rows st st.

Col C Work 2 rows st st.

Bobble patt

Col B Work 4 rows st st. Work row of bobbles thus: K3 (6) *mb, K9, rep from * to last 4 (7) sts, mb, K3 (6). Work 3 rows st st.

Col E Work 4 rows st st.

Double ridged eyelet patt

Col D

Rows 1 & 2 Knit.

Row 3 (RS) K2, *K2tog, yf, rep from* to last 3 sts, K3.

Row 4 K.

Rows 5 & 6 as rows 3 & 4.

Cloverleaf patt (multiple of 8 sts + 5).

Col F

Work 4 rows st st.

Row 5 K6 (7) *yf, sk2po, yf, K5, rep from * to last 1 (2) sts, K1 (2).

Row 6 Purl.

Row 7 K4 (5) *K3, yf, skpo, K3, rep from * to last 3 (4) sts, K3 (4).

Row 8 Purl.

Rows 9–12 St st.

Stripe patt

*** **Col D** Work 2 rows st st.

Col A K 1 row.

Col C Work 3 rows st st.

Col E Work 2 rows st st.

Diagonal stripe patt (strand cols *very loosely* across back of work)

Col B

Row 1 Knit.

Row 2 Purl.

68

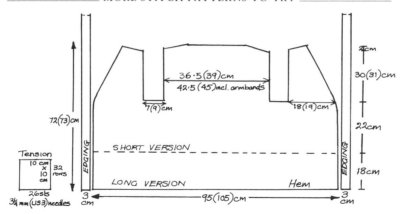

55 Measurement diagram—sleeveless jacket with padded picot edging

Row 3 *K3B, K2A, rep from * to last 2 (3) sts. K2 (3) B.

Row 4 P0 (1) A, *P3B, P2A, rep from * to last 2 sts, P2B. Work 4 more rows, moving diagonal 2 st stripe 1 st further to the right on every K row & 1 st further to the left on every P row, i.e. 6 rows stripe in total.

Row 9 Knit.

Row 10 Purl.

Dec Row

Col C K7 (9) *K2tog, K9, rep from * to last 9 (11) sts, K2tog, K7 (9) 225 (249) sts.

Col E Work 3 rows st st.

Col D K1 row.

Divide for back and fronts

P47 (50), cast off 18 (24), P95 (101), cast off 18 (24). P to end.

Cont on last set of 47 (50) sts for RF, working 2 row chevron patt (multiple of 13 sts + 2), changing col as foll work 4 rows F, 2D, 4B, 2C, 2E, 4A, 2E, 4C, 2E, 4D.

Row 1 K3 (5), *K2, m1, K4, sk2po, K4, m1, rep from * to last 5 (6) sts, K5 (6).

Row 2 Purl.

Rep these 2 rows throughout and rep col sequence as set, dec 1 st at beg of next and every foll 4th row to 30 sts, keeping patt and No. of sts correct, i.e. occasional neck edge inc still needed to counteract chevron patt dec.

Cont straight until armhole measures 30 (31) cm 11¾ (12¼)″—or measurement required, ending with a P row.

Shoulder shaping (short row sloped method)

K20 sts, *yf, s1P, yb, return sl st to LH needle.

Turn, P to end of row *. K10 sts.

Rep from * to *. K to first sl st.

** Pass sl st with bar to RH needle.

With LH needle pick up bar and return sl st to LH needle. K these 2 sts tog. **

K to next sl st. Rep from ** to **.

K to end of row. Cast off.

LEFT FRONT

Join yarn to sts for LF and work to match RF, i.e., dec 1 st at end of 3rd and every foll 4th row until 30 sts rem.

Cont straight until armhole matches that of RF, ending at armhole edge.

Shoulder shaping

K1 row. P 20 sts, *yb, s1P, yf, return sl st to LH needle. Turn.

K to end of row*. P10 sts. Rep from * to *.

P to first sl st. **Pass sl st with bar to RH needle.

With LH needle pick up bar and return sl st to LH needle. P these 2 sts tog **.

P to next sl st. Rep from ** to **.

P to end of row. Cast off.

BACK

Join yarn to centre 95 (101) sts for back, and cont in chevron patt as on fronts.

Row 1 K1 (4) *K2, m1, K4, sk2po, K4, m1.

Rep from * to last 3 (6) sts, K3 (6).

Work straight without shaping, changing cols as before until back matches fronts to shoulders, ending with a P row.

Shape shoulders

K to last 10 sts. *yf, s1P, yb, return sl st to LH needle. Turn * P to last 10 sts *yb, s1P, yf, return sl st to LH needle. Turn. * K to last 20 sts.

Rep from * to * as on last K row.

P to last 20 sts. Rep from * to * as on last P row. K to last 30 sts.

Rep from * to * as on last K row.

P to last 30 sts.

Rep from * to * as on last P row.

K to last 30 sts.

**Pass sl st with bar to RH needle.

With LH needle pick up bar and return sl st to LH needle.

K these 2 sts tog **.

K to next sl st.

Rep from ** to **. K to next sl st.

Rep from ** to **. K to end of row.

Cast off 30 sts. P to last 30 sts. ** Pass sl st with bar to RH needle. With LH needle pick up bar and return sl st to LH needle.

P these 2 sts tog. **

P to next sl st. Rep from ** to **. P to next sl st. Rep from ** to **. P to end of row.

Cast off rem sts.

MAKING UP

It is essential to block out main knitted body piece before making up (see page 151).

Hem

Fold jacket hemline to inside along picot edge and stitch down flat.

Armbands

Join shoulder seams.

Using size 2¾ mm circular needle, and col A, pick up & K 13 sts for every 16 rows around armholes, ignoring cast off edges at underarm. 166 (172) sts approx.

Work 7 rows st st, ending with a P row.

With col C, work 4 rows st st.

Next row, (RS) K2, *yf, K2tog, rep from * to last or last 2 sts, K1 or K2, according to No of sts picked up.

Work 3 rows st st.

Fold work in half across holes to form picot edge.

Next row With col A, *K1, at same time catch in horizontal bar of st from opposite inside edge of fold to make ridge.

Rep from * to end of row.

Cont in st st for 7 rows.

Cast off loosely.

Neck and front edging

Proceed as for armbands, picking up 330 (342) sts approx for short version of jacket, and 420 (432) sts approx for long version.

Padded edgings

Cut 1 × 5 cm (2″) width strip of terylene wadding to fit total all round length of neckline and front edging. Approx 115 cm (45¼″) length for shorter jacket, 150 cm (59″) for longer version. Make join at back neck if necessary. Cut 2 × 5 cm (2″) strips to fit armbands, approx 70 cm (27½″) long. Roll wadding strips lengthwise and place inside folded neck/front and armhole edgings. Stitch down edgings to inside of jacket, enclosing rolled up wadding. Stitch down both ends of finished armbands neatly to cast off edges of underarm.

Variations

Use this basic pattern shape to try out your own favourite stitch patterns in any sequence, changing colour, yarn and/or pattern every few rows.

TIPS

- First work a tension strip for each pattern, or take a chance and design as you go.
- Keep to approximately the same yarn weight throughout (4 ply or equivalent).
- The tension of individual stitch patterns will vary, but discrepancies are usually slight enough not to matter when knitting in narrow bands only. Avoid patterns which close up or pull in greatly, for example, cable or rib, and compensate for stranded colourwork, which tends to pull in, by using larger needles if necessary.
- Plan stitch repeats so that left-over stitches are split equally at row ends.
- Consider limiting yourself to one yarn or colour only, letting the stitch patterns alone provide the focal point of interest. Understated designs often have a simple elegance in complete contrast to the exuberance of wildly multi-coloured and textured knits.

Section 2
COLOUR

10

How to mix colour in theory

Many knitters lack the confidence to work out their own colour schemes, mainly because they haven't the faintest idea where to begin. Very few adults seem to have an instinctive 'feel' for colour, although as children we nearly all start off with a wonderfully lively, free and unrestrained colour sense. You have only to look at all those vibrant children's paintings on any primary school classroom wall to see the potential of the untrained mind as far as colour is concerned. But sadly, most adults retain little of that initial joyful exuberance, and very often formal instruction in how to use colour constructively is only available to art college students who intend to pursue a career in art and design.

Using colour should be a joy, not a source of anxiety. We all have to decide what colour wallpaper will look right with the new living room carpet and curtains when we redecorate, and many women in particular find it difficult to make their minds up as to which colours go well together when choosing new clothes for a wedding outfit or holiday wardrobe. It's no wonder that mix-n-match co-ordinates sell so successfully—it means that all that agonizing over which colours 'look right' together is removed at a stroke. Nevertheless, there are still many skilled amateurs who manage to make us catch our breath with the beauty of what they achieve through their natural ability to use colour imaginatively in their everyday lives.

Notice how one front garden in a row of identical terraced houses stands out from all the others when it has been tended by a skilled gardener with a good eye for colour. It is not simply a matter of green fingers, but the ability to know instinctively where to plant a clump of flowering plants just where they will set off or counterbalance other plant colours best.

Professional designers learn all about colour theory during their training. Just as it helps them to have a set of rules to cling to initially, so you will also find it helpful to have guidelines in your early days of experimenting with colour. Gradually, as you become more confident, you will find yourself referring to the rules consciously less and less until they become second nature to you—soon, you just *know* what colours will work well together. You will also feel quite relaxed and confident about breaking the rules when it suits you. Eventually you will find you have complete confidence in your own colour judgement without the need for outside guidance, and the sky's the limit after that!

So here is a simple introduction to colour theory, and remember you can apply these same rules to other aspects of your lifestyle as well as to knitting. We will discuss the practical knitting applications in the next chapter.

COLOUR THEORY

It all begins with the colour wheel: divide a circle into six equal segments. There are only three basic colours—red, blue and yellow, called *primary* colours, from which all other colours are derived. Colour in the primary colours in alternate segments as shown overleaf.

When you mix two primaries together you form what are known as *secondary* colours:

blue and yellow = green
yellow and red = orange
red and blue = violet

Mix and colour in your secondary segments.

PRIMARY COLS

SECONDARY COLS

MONOCHROMATIC   ANALOGOUS   COMPLEMENTARY   TRIADIC

COLOUR SCHEMES

56 Basic colour theory

Hues

All colours we have referred to so far are called hues, meaning that they refer to one colour as distinct from another, for example, blue as distinct from yellow.

Value

Colour value refers to the lightness or darkness achieved by mixing a colour with neutral white, grey or black to produce *tints*, *tones* or *shades* of the basic colour hue. (Neutrals are sometimes called *achromatic colours*.) For example:

white (neutral)	+ red (hue)	= pink *tint*
grey	+ red	= pinkish grey *tone*
black	+ red	= brown *shade*

Chroma

The chroma is the strength or weakness of a colour. 'Wishy washy' or very intense colours are achieved by diluting the amount of pure hue in a colour—in water colour paint this would be achieved by adding very little, or plenty of water according to the strength of colour you wished to produce.

Of course, you cannot mix coloured yarns together in quite the same way as paint, but in the next chapter you will see how you can still apply these principles to your coloured knitting and 'paint with yarns'.

BASIC COLOUR SCHEMES

Monochromatic

The use of tints, tones and shades of one colour only (simple, subtle and effective to use).

Analogous (Adjacent)

The use of neighbouring colour segments on the wheel. These schemes are more colourful than monochromatic but still subtle—my favourites, in fact.

Complementary

The use of colours that are opposite or practically opposite each other on the wheel. They are frequently used and very popular in many design situations and nature.

Triadic

The use of three colours equidistantly spaced around the colour wheel; such colours tend to look rather bright and garish in use. Triadic schemes can either look strikingly new or completely outdated, depending on what look is currently fashionable.

Polychromatic

The ultimate colour scheme using an unlimited number of colours together. (The 'no holds barred' approach! Get out your sunglasses to shield you from the glare!)

Whatever colour scheme you decide to use, you should also incorporate variations in value or chroma, as mentioned earlier.

DISTRIBUTION OF COLOUR

Pure colour is the most exciting and therefore tiring to the eye, so it is often wise to use your brightest colour in small doses and add the paler or more muted colours more lavishly.

Optical illusion, distance and surroundings

Some colours appear to advance or recede – for example, orange, yellow and red advance while violet and blue recede. Use this to create three-dimensional effects and make certain areas of colour appear to jump out at the viewer. The surroundings of each colour will also vary its individual impact. Neutral colours are useful for backgrounds as they do not detract from the more dominant colours of pattern motifs etc. In fact, they usually enhance them by failing to compete for our attention.

SYMBOLISM OF COLOUR

All colours have psychological and emotional undertones. Orange and red are warm colours because of their association with fire, whereas blues and greens are cool and tranquil—reminders of sky and grassy fields perhaps? Subconsciously, we are attracted to certain colours because of their associations, and these may even affect our moods one way or the other. This can be illustrated with examples of every day language which use colour terminology for this purpose, for example, 'black' moods, feeling 'blue', to see 'red', 'green' with jealousy, 'purple' with rage etc. On the whole, temperamental, fiery 'live wires' who love being the centre of attention will be attracted to red and bright colours generally, whereas quiet, unassuming people tend to choose muted pastels and neutrals, as might be expected.

Now to put your colour theory into practice.

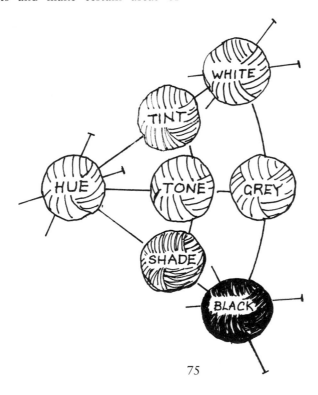

11

How to mix colour in practice

CHOOSING YOUR COLOURS

First of all, you must decide what type of colour scheme you are going to use. The simplest one is undoubtedly the *monochromatic* colour scheme: tints, tones and shades of one main colour only, together with variations in colour strength or intensity (chroma). So start with that and work on through all the schemes systematically. If your favourite colour is red, for example, this means that you may choose anything from the palest pink, cameo or rose *tint* to the deepest *shades* of red you can think of—claret, burgundy and maroon, perhaps. You may also use all the subtle *tones* like clover, camelia, dusty pink and mulberry as well as vibrant *hues* such as scarlet, crimson, poppy, flame or pillar box red to add punch.

You can see what a huge choice there is available within just one primary colour, and you have only to look at my household paint manufacturer's mix-n-match shade card if you need any more ideas. Of course, you could choose a neutral as your base colour, or alternatively one of the secondaries if you wish. How about purple used with lavender and aubergine?

Once you have decided in your mind, start building up a collection of actual yarns in your chosen colour scheme. This takes time so it is a good idea to think ahead to your next project while the previous one is still in progress. Begin with an empty basket in an odd corner of your home and gradually assemble a good selection of yarns by picking out one or two likely extras to add to the growing basketful every time you visit a woolshop.

I never buy more than one ball of each yarn at this stage—less painful on the pocket and much more fun to choose. I don't need to be so strict with myself either, and somehow I feel I have received much better value for my money buying ten *different* glorious shades and textures of yarn than I would have done with ten identical balls. Offset the cost of expensive 'fancies' by mixing in some cheaper plain yarns. Also remember to buy cut price oddments and use up any leftovers you have around the house.

Do not worry about matching dye lots—it is largely unnecessary with this approach to knitting where many different colours and textures are used together within one piece of knitting. It only matters when you knit up large areas in just one yarn because slight differences in shading draw attention to the joining row right across the garment.

When your basket starts brimming over with yarns you know you have enough to make a start, and anyway you can always add more later if necessary—either more variations of your chosen colour or repeats of some you have already used. At this stage you really can't be sure how much yarn will be needed in total. Living dangerously is half the fun of it, in fact! However, to reassure the more cautious knitters among you, approximate yarn quantities are given at the end of the book.

Carefully lay out all your chosen yarns in a shallow basket or tray in order to make up a sort of colour palette of yarns—rather like a paintbox, except that you will be using yarns instead of paint. Place different colours or tones next to each other until you strike upon a combination which pleases you. (Sometimes I make a colour winding as shown in Fig. 57 to get a quick impression of how the colours work together and what proportions of each I should use.) Then knit up a small experimental sample, either in basic stocking stitch,

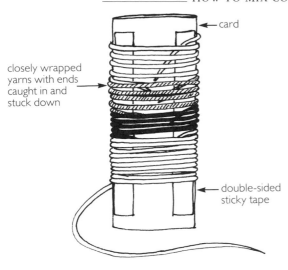

card

closely wrapped
yarns with ends
caught in and
stuck down

double-sided
sticky tape

57 Making a colour winding

or by utilizing a few of the stitches that you want in your finished design, mixing the yarn colours fairly freely at first until you achieve the desired effect.

When you first start, this tends to be a fairly random process, but as your knowledge increases you begin to learn from experience which stitches produce certain colour mixing effects readily, while others give a totally different result. It is surprising the extent to which stitch and colour effects vary according to the type of yarn used (see page 24).

You may find monochromatic colour schemes rather lacking in excitement. If you favour the use of at least two main colours, try out the *analogous* (adjacent) colour scheme next. Here you choose colours lying next to each other, blending tones of one colour gradually through to its neighbour on the colour wheel. If you choose green, for example, you might progress from emerald green, grass green, lime and citron, through to pure yellow, then back again through the yellowish greens to emerald again, so that a block of chevron knitted stripes knitted to and fro in this manner would produce waves of softly undulating and carefully blended colour.

In this case, it is important, when laying out your coloured yarns as before, to arrange them in the order in which you finally intend to knit them, so that you can check that the colours blend smoothly from one shade to the next. This can be achieved even more effectively if you use a slip stitch knitting

technique on the rows where you plan to change colour. This is explained in detail on page 80.

If your leanings veer towards a more adventurous use of colour, you will probably want to try one of the *complementary* colour schemes. Look around you and copy a few of nature's ideas. There is nothing to beat the impact of a bunch of bright purple and yellow pansies, for example; a prickly green holly bush with shiny red berries, or the more subtle green tones of a virginia creeper, its leaves tinged with deep red to forecast the return of autumn. Try interpreting this with several shades of green winter-weight yarn, shot through with rich flecks of red knitted in here and there to add eye-catching pinpoints of stitch interest and colour, the whole design held together visually with richer red knitted edgings which link the red pinpoints into a cohesive colour scheme.

Of course, if you have a 'no holds barred' attitude to colour, utilize it recklessly and riotously with a *triadic* or *polychromatic* colour scheme. Not for the faint hearted, these schemes are only for the fashion wardrobes of those who like to stand out in a crowd and make an impact come what may. Glory in your riotous and exhuberant love of vibrant colour—life will never be dull when you walk down the street in one of your knitted creations!

Whichever colour scheme you choose, it is helpful to decide on one particular ball of yarn as your main background or unifying colour. This will be used to tie your entire design together to give a complete creatively planned look, rather than just a jumble of colours, which simply confuse the eye and appear to have been thrown together without any forethought whatsoever. The easiest way to achieve this is to knit all your welts or edgings in this one chosen yarn only—that is, necklines, collars, button bands, armholes, cuff edgings, and lower edge welts, together with any pocket welts, tabs or belts.

And really that is all there is to it. So if you are already familiar with colour knitting techniques, try experimenting with a few knitted samples of your own now, and discover what a magnificent colour sense you've suddenly developed. Maybe you never knew you had it in you, but it was probably there all the time just waiting for you to unlock it. However, if you are raring to go, but are unfamiliar with the technicalities of changing colour in knitting, then turn the page and take it one step at a time, gradually trying out all the different colour knitting techniques for yourself.

12

Using your chosen colour scheme—colour knitting techniques

Inexperienced knitters generally find the thought of colour knitting rather exciting until they take a look at a typical multi-colour pattern with coded charts covered with meaningless symbols or endless row by row instructions; they then promptly freeze on the spot in terror! But it really is quite simple when you know how—it just *looks* difficult at first. The trick is to tackle it in easy stages. Don't let yourself be rushed, take things at your own pace and you will be racing through colour charts with the best of them in no time.

Try knitting this colour sampler which gradually introduces you to all the colour techniques you are ever likely to need. Practise each one until you feel at home with it, then proceed to the next until you have tried all of them.

COLOUR SAMPLER

The sampler is knitted mainly in 4 row bands of colour, working 3 rows of stocking stitch between each colour change RS row, but you can vary the width of stripes to suit yourself if you prefer. You will need 4 different coloured thickish yarns and 4 different coloured fine yarns which are roughly equivalent to the thick yarns when doubled together.

Using thick yarn, cast on 26 sts (or any even No.).

Work several rows st st, ending with a P row.

Simple horizontal stripes (fig. 60a)
To join in a new colour at the *start* of a RS row, insert RH needle into 1st st on LH needle in the usual way, and wrap loop from new ball of yarn around it, leaving end about 10 cm (4″) long hanging

down. K this stitch.

K next 2 or 3 sts double, using *both* ends of new yarn to secure firmly, then discard short end and K to end of row.

On next row make sure you treat the double stitches as single stitches. The old yarn end can either be broken off and darned neatly into the edge on back of knitting *or* if you will be using it again shortly, carry up side of work, twisting around new colour at end of row, to catch it in neatly until needed again.

Work several rows st st ending with RS facing ready for next col change row.

Weaving in ends as you work (fig. 60b) (saves hours of darning in ends with a needle)
With RS facing:
1 Grasping ends of both new and old yarn firmly with left hand, insert RH needle into 1st st on LH needle and wrap loop from new ball of yarn around it. K first stitch.
2 Insert RH needle into next st. Wrap two yarn ends up and over needle from back to front. Wrap new yarn round needle as if to knit in usual way. Unwrap the two yarn ends back over needle and complete the st by pulling it through.
3 K next st as normal.
4 Rep steps 2 and 3 until yarn ends are woven in securely for about 6 sts. Cut off ends and K to end of row. (This must be the most time saving tip I ever learnt. Practise until it becomes automatic—you will never regret it. It can also be used to change colour as many times as you like in the middle of a row).
Work several rows st st.

58 Colour knitting sampler

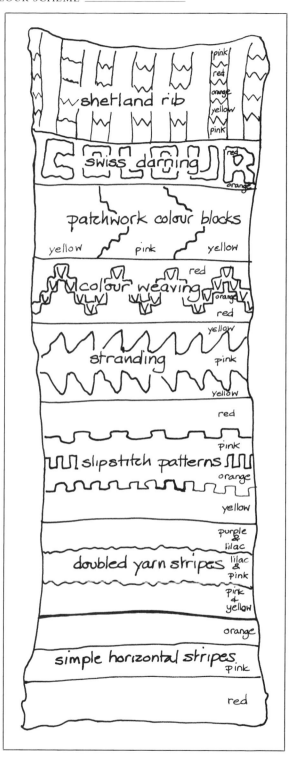

59 Key to colour knitting sampler

Two-colour doubled yarn stripes

Using 2 *fine* yarns doubled together as one (cols A & B), join in new cols as before and work several rows st st with cols A & B tog. Now discard col A and replace it by joining in 3rd col (C) so that you can now work several rows with cols B & C. Replace col B with 4th col (D) and work several rows with cols C & D.

This is a very easy way for relative beginners to make subtle, graduated colour changes. It also looks very effective in garter stitch.

Now change back to single, thicker yarns, remembering to treat double sts as single sts right across next row. Work 4 row simple horizontal stripe as before.

Slip stitch pattern 1

With new col

*K1, sl next st P wise.

Rep from * to end of row.

Work several rows st st.

Slip stitch pattern 2

(Slipping stitches over 2 rows causes a pulled texture which produces a more embossed effect.)

With new col:

(K1, sl 1) as before to end of row.

(sl 1, P1) to end of row.

Variations—try alternating position of slipped sections on K and P rows, or change sequence, e.g., (K2, sl2), (K3, sl1) etc.

Experiment to see which effect you like best.

Work several rows st st.

These simple slip stitch techniques are superb for analaogous (adjacent) colour schemes where one often wants to 'smudge' the colour changes to make them less obvious.

Stranding (figs 60c, d, e)

The traditional Fair Isle method of stranding uses only two colours per row. It seems intricate, but is not as difficult as it looks; it is suitable for small, regular pattern repeats, alternating the colours every few stitches and carrying the unworked colour loosely across the back of the work until it is needed again. The resulting double thickness fabric gives the knitting extra warmth. Stranding is more flexible than slip-stitch colour work and gives a flatter, more even texture. Modern colour-stranded patterns often use up to four colours per row, but only try two to start with, or you will get yourself in a terrible muddle if you are not used to the technique. Copy the chart shown on page 83, using the guidelines mentioned, or design your own on graph paper. Look at other geometric patterns for inspiration, for example, cross stitch embroidery samplers, oriental carpets, mosaics, etc.

Knit up to five stitches with the first colour, carrying the second colour loosely across the back of the work; do not pull the second yarn taut or the fabric will pucker. Then knit up to five stitches with the second colour, carrying the first colour loosely across the back of the work as before. Continue working with the colours alternately to end of row. Purl rows are worked in the same way, but with yarns at the front of the work.

If you are familiar with the continental method of knitting it is much quicker to work with the yarn held on the forefinger of both hands, rather than dropping and picking up each yarn every time you change colour. But this will take practice if you are not used to carrying the yarn with the left hand. You may find it easier to hold both yarns in the right hand, looped over both the forefinger and middle finger, flicking whichever yarn is required over the needle with the appropriate fingers.

If you combine both methods, theoretically you should be able to work with four yarns at once, two on the left hand and two on the right hand. A wonderful thought, but I have met very few knitters who can keep it up for any length of time as it demands skill and concentration. Congratulations, if you can manage it successfully. It is also now possible to buy a 'knitters' thimble', which incorporates thread guides enabling you to carry four colours at once on one forefinger.

Colour weaving (figs 60f, g)

Use this method for large pattern repeats of more than five stitches or when working with three or more colours in a row. It will keep the back of your work free from untidy loops of unworked yarn which might catch, pull or break. The technique is identical to that explained under 'Weaving in ends', but is used as an alternative method of carrying yarn at the back of the work (without breaking off the ends every time).

Holding one yarn in your right hand (to knit) and one yarn in your left hand, (to weave) knit first stitch in usual way. Insert right-hand needle into next stitch. Wrap the left-hand yarn up and over needle from back to front. Wrap right-hand yarn round needle as if to knit. Unwrap left-hand yarn back over needle and complete stitch by pulling it through in the usual way. Knit next stitch as normal. Repeat these two stitches alternatively to

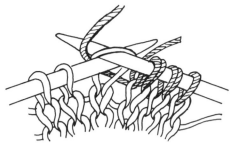

60a Joining in a new colour

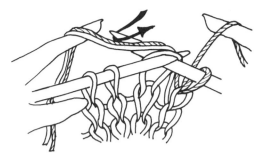

60b Weaving in ends

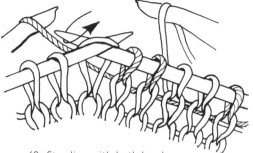

60c Standing with both hands

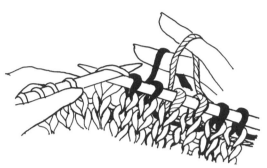

60d Standing with right hand

60f Colour weaving

60e Standing at back

60g Weaving at back

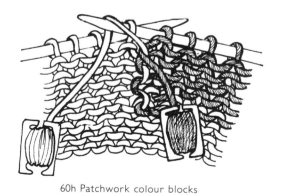

60h Patchwork colour blocks

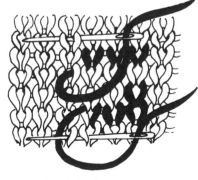

60i Swiss darning

60 Colour knitting techniques

81

weave spare yarn neatly in and out at the back of the work. It remains invisible to all intents and purposes from the right side. When the second colour is being worked, change and weave the first colour and vice versa as often as necessary.

The procedure is the same on purl rows except that the left-hand yarn is wrapped over needle from front to back, alternating the position of the yarn carried across each stitch on the previous row.

Patchwork colour blocks (Intarsia) (fig. 60h)

When working multi-coloured patterns with relatively large blocks of colour, stranding or weaving is unnecessary. Instead, the yarns are twisted round each other at each colour change to prevent holes forming, and left hanging at the back so that a single thickness fabric is formed. Divide each colour into small balls of yarn before you begin. You will need a separate one each time the colour changes across the row so you may need several balls of the same colour if it is used more than once in the same row.

The main problem is how to avoid the colours tangling at the back of the work, particularly if you are using a large number of balled yarns, which tends to slow progress down enormously. One solution is to wind manageable lengths of yarn onto bobbins, which you can buy or make yourself from stiff card. Make sure the working end of the yarn passes through the narrow opening.

Hang loaded bobbins at back of work. Alternatively, keep yarns in separate plastic bags secured loosely with an elastic band, or arrange in order of use in a shoebox, with holes in the lid, or divided up into separate sections. Or try using manageable lengths of *unwound* yarn so that there are no little balls to cause tangles and ends can simply be pulled free. This works well but you must join on new lengths of yarn more frequently. Use whichever method works best for you.

For vertical colour patterns the yarns will need to be twisted where the colour changes on every row. This method is not suitable for circular knitting as the different colours would always be found at the wrong end of each colour block to be knitted.

When patterns slant diagonally to the right, on right or wrong side, cross right-hand yarn in front of left-hand yarn and leave hanging, continuing with left-hand yarn. The yarns will loop together automatically on left slanting rows.

Swiss darning (fig. 60i)

This is a quick and easy method of adding colour to a piece of knitting after the main body of the knitting has been completed. It is really a form of embroidery which imitates knitting by covering the original knitted stitch with a new colour, and is particularly useful for simple motifs and small, detailed areas of colour. Many people find it easier than knitting with two or more coloured yarns at once, and it also has the advantage that no pre-planning is necessary. You can liven up a piece of plain knitting by placing a motif exactly where you want it, and are free to change your mind as often as you wish, unpicking and replacing colours when you grow tired of a particular motif or slogan. In addition, the double thickness fabric produced by swiss darning is useful for reinforcing garments subject to heavy wear, such as sweater elbows, children's dungaree knees, sock heels and toes, and fingers of gloves.

To work swiss darning on stocking stitch, thread a large, blunt-ended needle with yarn of similar thickness to that of background. Secure yarn at back of work. Insert needle at the base of the first stitch to be covered and push through to the front. Then insert it from right to left through the same stitch one row above.

Insert the needle once more into the base of the first stitch and bring it out at the front again, one stitch to the left, ready to repeat the process. If you look at the formation of the original knitted stitches carefully, you will soon be able to follow their path with ease in any direction. Do remember, however, to keep the tension of the new stitches the same as the stitches being covered. Simply follow the path of the original stitch with the new yarn and you are not likely to go wrong.

Shetland rib

This is a simple and effective colour technique used traditionally in Shetland knitting, when it is always knitted in the round rather than on two needles as used here.

With background colour and even number of stitches work several rows knit 2, purl 2 rib. Change colour every few rows on knit stitches only, continuing to purl stitches in background colour. For example:

Rows 1–4 With background yarn A work in K2, P2, rib.

Rows 5–8 (K2 B, P2 A) repeat to end.

Rows 9–10 (K2 C, P2 A) repeat to end.

Rows 11–22 With A (K2, P2) repeat to end.

Now cast off sampler in rib.

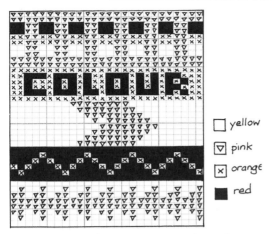

61 *Colour chart for upper section of sampler*

Key:
- ☐ yellow
- ▽ pink
- ☒ orange
- ■ red

COLOUR CHARTS

Instructions for colour knitting patterns are much easier to follow in visual chart form on graph paper than as written row by row instructions. Each square represents one stitch and a horizontal row of squares represents one row of knitting or one pattern repeat. The squares are coloured in according to the yarn colour required for each stitch; or different symbols are used for each colour if the chart is shown in black and white only (in which case, there will always be a key to the colour symbols used). The chart is usually worked in stocking stitch, starting from the bottom right-hand corner, so that all odd-numbered, knit rows are worked from right to left, and all even-numbered, purl rows are worked back from left to right. If you knit chart patterns in the round, remember to start *each* row from the right as you will always have the right side of the work facing towards you—this means you can see the pattern developing from the right side, so mistakes are easy to spot and can be rectified immediately.

If the pattern is repetitive, only one colour repeat is usually shown, with instructions to work as many times as necessary in order to complete the row, dividing any left over stitches equally between the beginning and end of the row to centralize the design.

You can easily work out your own colour charts on graph paper. Cross stitch and canvas work embroidery charts can just as easily be used for knitting, but remember that knitted stitches are not exactly square. The pattern will always look slightly 'squashed' from top to bottom unless you elongate

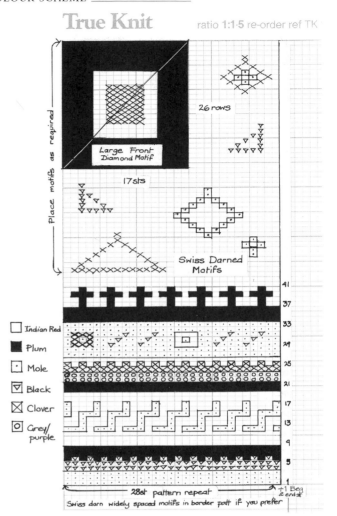

Key:
- ☐ Indian Red
- ■ Plum
- ⊡ Mole
- ▽ Black
- ☒ Clover
- ⊙ Grey/purple

62 *Colour chart for tunic length chevron sweater with long sleeves (see p. 140 and colour section)*

the pattern slightly. Alternatively, *knitters' graph paper* (see stocklist at back of book) which takes care of this, by elongating the squares to give a closer approximation to the actual stitch dimensions. It is available in several different sizes to match your own stitch/row tension ratio, and usually includes directions for working out which size you need from a tension square. Simply divide row tension by stitch tension to establish correct ratio size to use,

e.g. $\frac{26}{17} \simeq 1.5$

Practise these techniques on your colour knitting sampler until you are ready to try a colour knitting project of your own.

13
Picture knitting project

Now that you have all the main colour knitting techniques at your fingertips from the previous chapter (well, some of them, I hope, even if not all!) it's time to try out your new skills in a colour project of your own. The choice of subject, and the way you interpret it is really up to you. Yet, most knitters, however advanced, would freeze at the idea of thinking up original designs out of thin air without guidelines to help them. In no time at all, they would be sidling back to nice, safe, commercially-produced knitting patterns. So I suggest you begin by doing something rather closer to copying a pattern in the way you have been used to. But instead of copying you will be *interpreting* or *converting*. It is really halfway between copying and designing from scratch, and will help to give you confidence and ideas for future design projects of your own.

Choose a simple picture which you think might convert effectively into knitting. The picture will be your source of inspiration for a free style interpretation of your own, using colour knitting techniques. Leaf through any handy magazines and look for likely subjects. Greeting cards, postcards and photographs often provide rich source material too. Keep searching until you find something which looks suitable, and which also appeals to your personal taste. You want to enjoy what you are doing, or it will become just a boring exercise.

The subject can be anything from subtle, hazy landscapes to vibrant wild abstracts—it really doesn't matter. The choice is entirely yours.

However, try to choose something which won't cause too many problems to knit. Of course, you don't have to follow your picture in *every* detail anyway. Try and avoid anything too intricate and

precise. It is difficult to make figures look realistic, for example. This is why impressionist paintings are so perfect for our purposes; there are no hard edges, everything is smudgy and blurred. Just as the artist paints an *impression* of what he sees, you can knit your own impression in the same way.

Let me stress straightaway that I am not thinking of the picture sweaters that were fashionable several years ago, although of course you may knit like that if you wish. I am really suggesting that you knit your picture in a much freer way, and for this reason it is better not to transfer your chosen picture on to graph paper as it will take away the spontaneity of the project and delay the start of the actual knitting. 'What! No charts to guide us?' my students query disbelievingly at first. But in this case you have a picture to guide you instead—and you will learn a great deal more from looking at that than you would from a chart.

You see, you will need to study your picture very closely to discover what colours to use, and when you do you will find to your surprise that an object like a tree, for example, does not really consist of a single shade of green as so often seen in picture knits, but is made up of at least a dozen different green tints, tones and shades. This is quite apart from the other tinges of colour you can detect where the sun glints off the leaves, for example, or where certain areas are plunged into shadow, or reflect the light from nearby objects. With your new understanding of colour theory, it is now time to apply your knowledge practically.

If you are fairly new to knitting, you won't yet have acquired the huge bag of leftover yarns which no prolific knitter can avoid. If so, you may wish to restrict the number of colours used to cut down on

63 Picture knitting techniques (from top) stocking stitch, (lower left) colour winding in overlapping strips with added surface texture, (right) three-dimensional knitting applied to background of colour winding

unnecessary expense. But for the rest of you, try to pick out at least 20 or so colours for your picture, although only tiny oddments of each will be needed. You may still need to buy one or two extras, but do first rummage through fellow knitters' oddment bags as well if they will allow you. They may have just the shade you are looking for. Perhaps you could do a swap? Remember, too, that small hanks of tapestry wool or skeins of embroidery silk can also be incorporated, as can any of the unconventional yarn substitutes referred to in the texture section.

Ready with your pile of assorted colours? Right, let's get started. Cast on about 20 stitches or so in one yarn only, using the main background colour at the lower edge of your picture. Using your picture as your guide, start knitting from the bottom right-hand corner, working your way across to the bottom left-hand corner in stocking stitch or any other stitch which seems appropriate. Change colours as you need to, using any of the colour techniques you have already attempted from the last chapter. Remember, wrong side rows are worked from left to right.

85

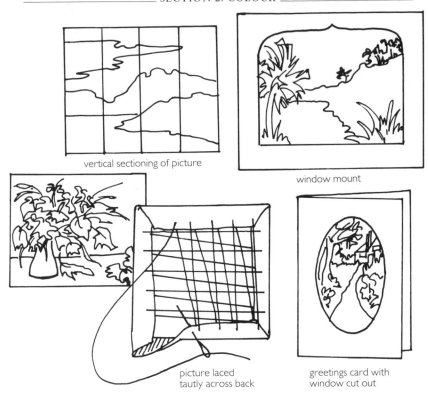

vertical sectioning of picture

window mount

picture laced
tautly across back

greetings card with
window cut out

64 Picture knitting project

If you find it difficult to decide how many stitches to knit in each colour across the row, divide your picture into four equal, vertical sections so you will know that each section of the row uses up one quarter of the stitches on your needle, i.e., 5 if you cast on 20 stitches. You will find that 20 stitches doesn't look very much and 40 produces a larger, more impressive piece of work, but you do need to concentrate a great deal at first, and all that colour changing slows up the pace enormously. It is much better to complete a small project successfully than to give up on a bigger one half way through because you don't seem to be getting anywhere and therefore lose heart before you have finished.

For a project such as this, where you are using so many colours at once, don't worry too much about what happens to your yarn ends. It's really not practical to worry about what is happening on the wrong side when you already have more than enough to cope with at the front! But if you use the finished picture in a context where the wrong side will be seen or worn as part of a garment, you will need to darn in your ends eventually. Otherwise, don't bother if the ends are not going to show. However, do remember to twist yarns around each other when changing colours in blocks, or you will find gaps appearing, particularly if the colours change in a vertical line somewhere in your picture.

Another thing, don't be put off if your first few rows resemble nothing more than a meaningless jumble of colour. If you cover up most of your source picture to expose only the equivalent of the rows you have already knitted, you will see that it also looks pretty meaningless! So don't despair, plough on, and all of a sudden you will realize your picture is starting to take shape. Keep going until you have completed the entire picture, or at least enough of it to form a pleasing composition in its own right, then cast off. Block out (see page 151) and lightly steam press on the wrong side, then stand back, take a good look, and admire your handiwork against a plain background.

Some of my students have managed to produce the most exquisite miniature pictures using the

65 *Picture knitting designed and made by Maureen O'Dwyer*

method described here (see colour section). The outstanding ones deserve to be framed and hung on the living room wall in pride of place. Others, while not masterpieces of design and technique, have served as useful introductions to creative colour knitting, leading on to bigger and better projects of various kinds later on. You could knit your own originally-designed, ceiling-height, wall hanging for example!

How to use your first miniature picture? Try cutting out a rough window in a piece of coloured paper and place it over your picture so that you see how much a correctly cut board mount and frame contributes to your finished piece of knitting. Makes quite a difference, doesn't it? If it really looks promising, you can have your work mounted and framed professionally. But it is really not that difficult to do yourself with the aid of some mounting board (available from art and craft shops) a sharp craft knife, metal ruler, well sharpened pencil and a steady hand.

Choose a neutral or toning colour for your background mount and decide how big you want your finished mount to be, perhaps to fit an existing empty frame which is already available. Measure out, mark lightly with the pencil and cut to size with the craft knife, using the metal ruler to give a good, clean edge. Cover up the working area of your mount with your ruler when cutting, to protect against accidental slips of the knife which might score the mount in the wrong place by mistake, and

remember to place an old piece of card underneath your cutting area if you are using the dining room table!

Mark out a central window in your mount, slightly smaller than the dimensions of your knitting after blocking (3–5 mm ($\frac{1}{8}$–$\frac{1}{4}$″) less all round) leaving a slightly larger surround underneath your window than at the top and sides so that the picture doesn't look top heavy. Stretch the knitted picture taut by lacing to and fro across the back of a piece of card with strong thread, or simply fix to the back of the window mount with double-sided sticky tape, which is much quicker but looks rather less professional.

Alternatively, you could use your picture to make a special greetings card. Fold a piece of thin card in half. Cut your window mount in the front and paste your knitted picture inside so that the knitting is framed by the front cover of the card where it is seen through the window whether the card is open or closed. Simple and effective. If you would rather use your finished picture in a more practical context, then how about turning it into an eye-catching pocket on a plain knitted sweater, jacket or cardigan? Or even on a knitted hat? Other simple multi-coloured items you can knit without worrying unduly about shaping are bags, scarves, belts, shawls, headboard and window seat covers,

66 Alternative project ideas

67 Sampler sweater

patchwork blankets, pram covers, wall hangings, and cushions of all sizes.

For a simple shoulder bag cast on about 60 stitches or so with size 4 mm (US 6) needles. Knit straight up using any combination of coloured stripes, traditional fair isle patterns, etc. until the work measures double the length you want the finished bag to be. Cast off. Fold the bag in half and knit, stitch or crochet the sides together. Add a length of french knitting or a twisted or plaited cord (you could combine the two) for a shoulder strap, and attach at each end to the sides of the bag—either at the top edge or covering up any less than perfect seams down the sides of the bag. Add a tassel or two if you like, or maybe a fringe. Perhaps you can think of some other simple knitting project ideas or how about working a larger design on the front of a child's rectangular sweater? Instructions for other simple knitting projects are included at the end of Chapter 16.

Once you have worked through the whole of this section on colour you may find you have built up so much confidence about mixing colours that you no longer need to stick to the rules. Rules are made to be broken once you know what you are doing. By now you may well have developed the instinctive use of colour which every designer learns.

Samples of picture knitting by (from top left working clockwise) *Sheila Ryle, Jane Meade, Alison Jabs, Dilys McIntyre, Kate Sendles, Jan Pattinson, Pauline Knight* (centre) *Marie Holmes.*

Fitted silk sweater with pointed welts.

All-in-one chevron-shaped sweater with long sleeves shown in differing textures and colours.

Raglan-sleeved tunic-length chevron sweater mainly in cotton chenille DK weight.

Sleeveless chevron sweater in DK weight cotton.

Multi-colour coat – ideas using draped and gathered effects.

Cardigan variation of chevron sweater, knitted by Sheila Ryle.

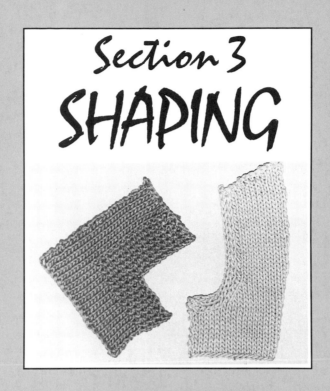

Section 3
SHAPING

14

Importance of Tension

How many of you—beginners or experienced knitters alike—ever bother to knit up a tension sample before launching into your latest knitting pattern? Precious few, I suspect. Most knitters are far too keen to get started on an actual garment to waste time on what they see as unnecessary details, blithely assuming that their tension is average and that if they follow the pattern instructions given for their size then the finished result will be bound to fit them. Anyway, they reason, with the baggy fashions of recent years it doesn't matter very much if it turns out slightly bigger or smaller than expected.

But alas, that happy state of affairs is now coming to an end with the gradual return of more body conscious fashions which need to fit correctly to look right. So tension samples will become vital once again, together with a more accurate understanding of how tension and fit are related.

For the would-be designer this is even more important, because her approach is quite different from that of a knitter who is trying to match her tension to that of an existing pattern. The designer creates her own tension rather than following someone else's, so she needs a tension sample to work out how to convert the measurements planned for her new design into stitch and row numbers.

SO WHAT IS TENSION?

Tension is simply a measure of the tightness or looseness of a piece of knitted fabric, expressed in terms of the number of stitches and rows in a given measurement.

MAKING A TENSION SAMPLE

When following a pattern knit up a sample at least 10 cm (4″) square, using the yarn, needle size and stitch pattern specified. Cast on slightly more than the number of stitches required for 10 cm and knit enough rows to complete a square. Cast off, pin out slightly stretched, and lightly press the sample. Then, using a ruler, mark out a 10 cm square on the knitting with pins. Carefully count the number of stitches and rows between the pins, making sure you include any half or quarter stitches and rows. The odd fractions can make quite a difference to the finished size. Check your figures against the pattern tension: if you have too many stitches or rows to

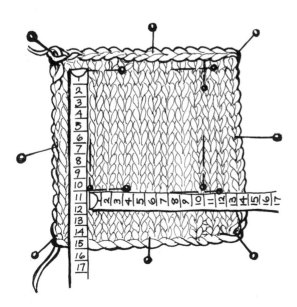

68 Measuring tension

91

10 cm then your tension is too tight and you should try again using needles one size larger; if too few, your tension is too loose, so try needles one size smaller. For complex lacy stitch patterns where it is difficult to count accurately, add thread markers before and after a specific number of stitches and rows, for example, over two complete pattern repeats, and calculate your tension from these figures instead. Only when you have adjusted your own tension to match that of the pattern can you be reasonably sure that your knitting will produce the measurements stated, although you can often adjust incorrect row tension later when knitting the actual garment.

By now beginners will understand why so many knitters are tempted to miss out this stage! It's hardly the most thrilling aspect of knitting.

DESIGNING YOUR OWN FABRIC AND TENSION SAMPLES

When you start designing your own patterns you must not only create the tension on which the garment measurements will be based, but also the design for the fabric structure itself, which is a much more exciting process. Small test samples or 'swatches' are therefore the quickest and easiest way to find out which fabric designs both feel right and look good, with all kinds of experimental combinations of yarn, texture, colour and stitch pattern being tried in the quest to produce something new and original. Various design resources may be used for inspiration, or ideas may be tried out simply at random; designers often knit up lots of these experimental samples before hitting upon the exact effect desired, often stumbling across something completely different but fascinating by chance. The best ideas will then be sized up and developed into full size garments by designing shapes around the fabric created, using the designer's own tension to calculate the number of stitches and rows required.

Try it for yourself and you'll soon find that knitting up swatches can be one of the most exciting parts of the design process. The sheer pleasure of creating your own successful knitted fabric designs is hard to beat. You may have discovered this already if you've tried out some of the ideas suggested as starting points earlier in the book. If not, now's the time to begin; it won't take you long to create something original if you plunge in freely, without letting rigid preconceptions hold you back.

69 *Comparing tension – both these shapes are 28 stitches wide and 40 rows deep*

HOW TO START

Remember that tension varies a great deal according to needle size, yarn thickness, texture, colour, and stitch pattern; you'll need to consider how these affect each other if you are to create a fabric which has reasonable elasticity and holds its shape well (see page 24). Use the recommended needle size given on most yarn ball bands as a guide, although you can vary this to suit yourself, according to the effect you want.

The average stocking stitch tension for the yarn concerned will also be given. This will help you decide how many stitches to cast on for a tension sample at least 12 cm (4¾") square. The stitch tension will alter according to the stitch pattern used, so if you change from one stitch pattern to another throughout, you may need to increase or decrease your stitch numbers accordingly. For example, rib and cable patterns pull the work in so you must add

70 Designing your own tension swatches

more stitches, whereas lacy patterns and garter stitch spread out widthways needing fewer stitches. Alternatively, alter your yarn thickness or needle size to achieve the same result, and use these factors to help you mix thick and thin yarns successfully, or plain and fancy ones. It's all a matter of experimenting and learning from your results. You'll discover other things along the way too—for example, that it's best not to overload your design with too much going on at once. Fancy textures or multi-colour patterns usually work best with simple shapes; plainer patterns are good with complicated shapes. The possibilities are endless, and you could spend a lifetime discovering just a few of them.

Work enough rows to complete a square or show a representative sample of your fabric design, then cast off. Count the number of stitches and rows to

10 cm (4″) as before, and label your swatch with these tension details together with the needle size for future reference.

Of course, once you've got over the shock of your first success, you'll want to go on to the next stage and convert your test sample into a full size design. The following chapters will show you how to construct a variety of garment shapes. Remember that the time spent sampling always saves time in the end. No more struggling to match someone else's tension—you work to your own tension from now on, and it's always better to knit up a small sample and work out accurate stitch and row calculations from that than launch blindly into your first sweater design with only the vaguest notion what size it will end up.

Convinced? Then let's move on . . .

15

How to plan design shapes

ADAPTING COMMERCIAL PATTERNS

ADAPTING COMMERCIAL PATTERNS

You may prefer to start off by adapting commercial patterns to build up your confidence before plunging into your first design proper. You can do this in a number of different ways:

Yarn substitution

It is important to match the tension of the original yarn as closely as possible if you are to have any hope of producing the same size and shape of garment as that shown in the pattern. So keep to the same type of yarn weight and texture category, for example, double knitting weight or mohair texture, and compare the ballbands if possible to see if the length measurement per ball is roughly compatible. This will also help you to estimate whether you need more or less balls of yarn than originally required, for example, synthetic yarns usually weigh less, so go further. Of course, it goes without saying that you will need to knit up a tension sample and adjust needle sizes to match tension if necessary.

Changing stitch pattern

This can change the look of a style completely. Check the tension of the original stitch pattern and knit up a tension sample of any other pattern you like to match this tension. Any knitting stitch dictionary gives hundreds of possible choices or try one of those suggested in Chapter 9. Remember, however, that certain patterns pull in much more than others (see page 92) so it's probably best to choose a pattern of the same basic type as the original. For example, lace patterns will not be suitable substitutes for cable patterns. This can also be a useful way of livening up a plain stocking stitch design.

Lengthening or shortening a pattern

Check the pattern measurements against your own and decide where alterations need to be made. Length alterations in the main body are usually made somewhere between the lower edge and armholes to avoid unnecessary complications with shaping. If the pattern pieces are straight it is simply a matter of adding or subtracting the number of rows required according to the tension. Adjust this to the nearest complete repeat if you are using an intricate stitch pattern, and remember to adjust each pattern piece by the same amount so that seams will match up accurately. Minor fitted sleeve adjustments are made in the straight section after the increasing and before the sleeve head shaping begins. (See Chapter 19 for how to make length adjustments in shaped areas.)

Altering a neckline

You can change the look of a pattern completely by revamping the neckline. It is a simple matter to turn a round neck into a polo neck by continuing to knit round and round upwards until you reach the polo neck depth required, or work to and fro from the centre front for a simple roll collar instead. You can also substitute a shaped round neck for a straight slash neck, or add a V or square neckline if you prefer. Experienced knitters will have followed all these procedures many times in the past so should not find it too difficult to tackle changes on their own. (See Chapter 18 for guidance.)

Adding panels and borders

This can be an easy way of individualizing a pattern without having to do any extra stitch calculations because you can use the same yarn and therefore

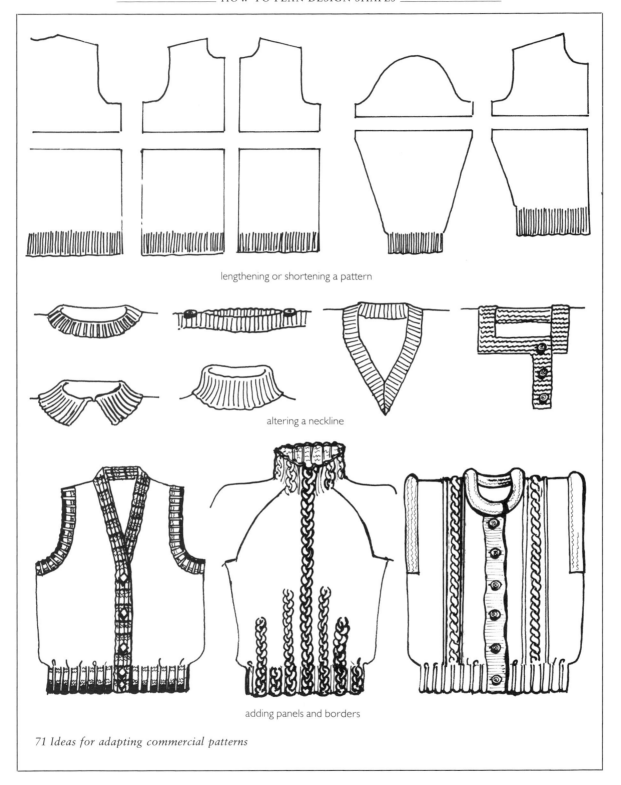

lengthening or shortening a pattern

altering a neckline

adding panels and borders

71 Ideas for adapting commercial patterns

work to the same tension as the original pattern, simply changing colours for your border with a contrast stripe or multi-colour pattern. It may even be acceptable to use a stitch pattern with a markedly different stitch tension (but try to keep to the original row tension) if you add a narrow vertical panel which will not affect the width of the garment enough to distort the shaping—a cable panel down the middle of a plain sweater for instance, or even cables down both sides of a sweater front or cardigan if you add a few stitches extra to compensate for the loss of width. Place your panels so that they extend into the shoulder area to avoid any difficulties with the neck shaping if you have altered the stitch numbers.

With all these adaptations it is reassuring to know that you have a tried and tested pattern to fall back on if you come up against any problems. This enables you to build up your confidence in easy stages so you gradually become bold enough to tackle more and more aspects of the design process on your own.

PLANNING YOUR OWN DESIGN SHAPES

Getting ideas down on paper
There are several ways you can start planning design shapes from scratch, but whatever method you choose, don't be too ambitious to begin with. Quick results are needed to boost your confidence, so for your first design pick an uncomplicated test swatch, knitted with fairly thick yarn and needles, and jot down your ideas for it on paper together with a rough sketch of the style you have in mind. It doesn't matter if you can't draw; it's only for your own reference. Plan a simple shape only; complex designs can come later. Don't get too technical or use wildly expensive yarns either; if you're worrying about yarn costs you'll be tense before you start. But with a good selection of colour co-ordinated leftovers from your oddment bag you'll feel you

have nothing to lose and everything to gain if things work out well. You'll also need a tape measure, a notebook for pattern calculations, and a pocket calculator if your arithmetic is shaky.

Taking body measurements and allowing for ease
It is vital to take accurate body measurements as shown if you want your finished design to fit well. Then decide how much extra you want to allow for ease of movement. This is the difference between body and finished garment measurements and determines the tightness or looseness of the fit. Measure a favourite sweater and compare it with your own body measurements if you're not sure how much ease to allow.

Notice that tightly fitting garments require negative ease—that is, they measure less than the corresponding body measurements and stretch to fit the body.

Fine yarns require less ease than thick yarns, and garments worn next to the body require less than over garments. The amount of ease also varies according to current fashion. Compare the baggy fashions of recent years with the fitted styles of the 50s which now look right up to date again. However, we have grown so used to the comfort of loosely fitting garments that they will probably remain popular for some time yet. Measure yourself carefully, or get a friend to help, noting down a complete list of measurements in your pattern notebook. Remember to update the list if necessary before using it again on future projects. You will only need very few body measurements for basic rectangular shaped garments.

Measurement diagrams
Whether you're the type of person who scribbles ideas on the back of an envelope or prefers to set things out in intricate detail, you will need to make some sort of measurement diagram in order to show the shape of your garment design clearly. A plan of the spread out garment pieces with detailed measurements is best.

EASE ALLOWANCES

	Tight	Close fitting	Standard	Loose	Oversized
Bust/chest & hip sizes	− 4 to5 cm ($-1\frac{1}{2}$ to 2″)	− 2 to + 2 cm ($-\frac{3}{4}$ to $\frac{3}{4}$″)	+ 5 cm (+ 2″)	+ 10 to 12 cm (+ 4 to $4\frac{1}{2}$″)	+ 13 cm up (+$5\frac{1}{2}$″ up)
Wrist, upper arm & armhole sizes	− 5%	0%	+ 10%	+ 25%	+ 40%

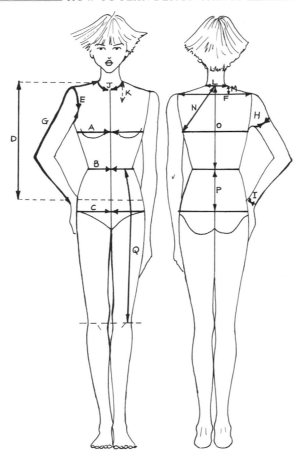

72 Body measurements

KEY TO MEASUREMENT DIAGRAMS

* denotes basic measurements required for
rectangular shaped garments

  *A *Bust/chest—around fullest part, not allowing
    tape to slip lower at back.*
  B *Waist—around natural waistline.*
  C *Hip—around fullest part approximately 20 cm
    (8″) from waistline.*
  *D *Finished length of garment from top bone in
    spine to lower edge (av. 60 cm/23½″).*
  *E *Armhole depth—measure from top of shoulder
    around underarm and back up to shoulder,
    then halve the total.*
  *F *Shoulder to shoulder—back width from
    armhole to armhole.*
  *G *Neck to wrist—Top bone in spine to wrist
    taking tape over shoulder.*

  *H *Upper arm—around fullest part
    (av 25 cm/10″).*
  I *Wrist.*
  J *Around neck—touching collar bone at front.*
  K *Front neck depth—from top of shoulder to
    desired front neckline depth.*
  L *Neck width—desired width of back neckline
    (av 15 cm/6″).*
  M *Shoulder depth—top bone in spine to shoulder
    to shoulder line.*
  N *Neck to underarm—top bone in spine to
    required top of side seam according to style.
    (Add ⅕ of total bust ease allowance.)*
  O *Back neck to waist.*
  P *Waist to hip.*
  Q *Skirt length.*

Converting measurements into stitches and rows

Basing your calculations on the tension taken from your test swatch, divide the number of stitches and rows per 10 cm/4″ by 10 if using centimetres, or 4 if using inches, to establish the tension per cm/″ which is easier to use for most calculation purposes. Then multiply all the measurements on your plan by either the stitch or row tension—that is, if the garment is to be knitted from the bottom up then all widthways measurements will be in stitches, and all vertical measurements in rows. If knitted horizontally from cuff to cuff, convert vertical measurements to stitches and horizontal measurement to rows.

Pattern repeats

These must be allowed for when planning designs, for example, a 10 st repeat will not fit exactly into an 86 st row. Split the remainder equally:

e.g., 8 repeats of 10 sts with 3 odd stitches over at each end of the row. *Or* adjust the stitch numbers slightly to obtain an exact number of repeats, although this will slightly alter your finished measurements:

e.g., 9 repeats of 10 stitches = 90 sts per row instead of 86.

Seam allowances

Add 1–2 sts extra to the stitch totals for seam allowances on each pattern piece, according to whether you prefer to sew up seams a half or full stitch in from the edges.

Estimating yarn requirements

It's always difficult to estimate how much yarn you will need for a project, because you cannot know for certain until you've finished knitting it, and by then you will already have made your decisions. Of course, a mixed yarn project is easier because you don't have to worry about matching dye lots, and even if you cannot obtain more of a yarn you can simply add in something else which blends in colour, texture and yarn weight. But for a design using one yarn only there are various ways of estimating *approximate* yarn quantities at least.

1 You can weigh a similar garment or look at a pattern resembling your design and buy the yarn quantity stated, preferably using the same yarn and colour (differing dye intensities make even different shades of the same yarn vary in weight). Compare the length measurement per ball if stated on the ball bands. This gives a more accurate guide than weight alone.

2 Knit up one ball of yarn. Multiply the height by the width and divide the area of knitting produced into the approximate area of the entire garment as calculated from your measurement plan, roughly converting each pattern piece into rectangular shapes for easy calculation. This will give you the approximate number of balls needed to complete your garment.

3 Calculate the number of stitches knitted from one ball by multiplying the number of stitches per row by the number of rows knitted. Calculate the number of stitches in the back and one sleeve in the same way, by using your measurement diagram, and double the result. Divide one into the other as above.

4 Keep a check on the number of balls used to knit the back and one sleeve. Approximately the same amount will be needed to complete the rest of the garment, not including edgings.

Always over-estimate and allow an extra ball for safety if possible. Keep a record of how much yarn is used for each project, together with a ball band and snippet of yarn for future reference. This may help to make future estimates easier.

Summary of the design process

1. Choose your yarn(s) and needles.
2. Choose appropriate stitch pattern(s).
3. Knit up experimental tension samples.
4. Measure tension and label clearly.
5. Jot down rough sketch on paper.
6. Take body measurements.
7. Add ease allowances.
8. Make measurement diagram with plan of pattern pieces.
9. Mark relevant measurements on plan.
10. Convert measurements into stitches and rows using tension sample.
11. Add seam allowances.
12. Estimate your requirements.

If your design is a simple one, consisting only of rectangular shapes, you will now be ready to start knitting. See Chapters 16 and 18 for detailed instructions, examples and ideas for design projects using simple rectangles and fitted shapes.

Shaped garments may require a further stage to cope with the curved sections of the pattern. Choose any of the following methods:

Graph paper or tension grid method

Relevant pattern sections are drafted onto paper in chart form using one square per stitch. See page 117. This is the method chosen by most professional designers for maximum accuracy, and is often used in combination with mathematical calculations. However, knitting stitches are rarely square— usually wider than they are tall, causing shape distortion when normal square graph paper is used. So, specified knitters' graph paper is now available in various ratio grids to give a truer representation of the design shape being charted. To select the correct grid, simply divide the number of rows per 10 cm (4″) by the number of stitches:

$$e.g. \quad \frac{28 \text{ rows}}{22 \text{ sts}} = 1.27 = 1.4 \text{ or} \quad \frac{24 \text{ rows}}{16 \text{ sts}} = 1.5$$

so choose 1:1.4 grid   *so choose* 1:1.5 grid

Paper pattern method

A full size paper pattern is made to body measurements, or a made up garment or dressmaking pattern (without darts or seam allowances) is used as a template. Calculate cast on stitches and knit to shape, checking work frequently against pattern. For complicated shapes a calico 'toile'— that is, a full size 'cut and sew' prototype garment— may be made to check the fit and hang of the garment before superimposing a tension grid onto the pattern pieces for greater accuracy.

Shape as you knit

This is a trial and error method for impetuous souls who hate advance planning or have a complete mathematical mental block. Simply hold the knitting up against you as you work, shaping by inspired guesswork. Fast, fun, but very risky. Not to be recommended unless other methods seem too much bother and you know it's the only way you'll ever get around to designing anything for yourself! Anyway, if it doesn't work you can always unravel it and start again. However, this won't happen if you follow the steps mentioned earlier, so you must decide for yourself whether gambles to save time are really worth the risk. Extra care and effort usually pays off best in the long run.

16
Simple rectanglar and square shapes

The mere thought of working out your own shaping methods for knitwear can be daunting at first, so it is no wonder that simple rectangular shapes consisting only of straight lines and unshaped sections have proved so enormously popular with knitters of all types. Rectangles are easy to plan, make and fit because there are no complications with curves and diagonal lines, these being features which demand a more advanced knowledge of correct shaping technique to accomplish successfully. Rectangles also provide a good basis for designs that concentrate mainly on the use of texture and colour for impact, since the shape is unlikely to distract attention from the more dominant features of the design. The elasticity of knitting also means that a simple rectangular sweater in a standard size will stretch comfortably to fit a variety of different figure shapes.

So gather together any promising tension swatches you've knitted up already and start planning your first complete sweater design project, working through the design process as summarized on page 98. Use these examples as a guide for your own calculations:

EXAMPLE A (see page 102)

(steps 1–3)
Start with a simple garter stitch tension swatch knitted on size 4 mm (US 6) needles, using two strands of 4 ply plain wool yarn in mixed colours with a softly blended random colour effect achieved by interchanging the colours every few rows (see page 80) and fig. 45.

4 Tension = 20 sts $\left.\right\}$ to 10 cm (4″)
38 rows

5 Make a rough sketch of your design.
6 Take relevant body measurements: e.g.,
Bust measurement 87 cm (34″).
Finished garment length 50 cm (19$\frac{3}{4}$″)
Armhole depth (halved) 20 cm (8″) approx. incl. ease.
Neck width 25 cm (10″) approx. incl. ease
This top is simply two rectangles sewn together, so only the bust measurement is really necessary. Leave the finished garment length and dimensions for neck and armhole openings until later if you prefer, measuring the knitting up against you as you work.
7 Add 5 cm/2″ ease around the bust for a standard fit or 10 cm/4″ for a roomier garment, e.g., 87 + 5 = 92 cm (34 + 2 = 36″)
8 Draw a measurement diagram of the front/back. Both pattern pieces are identical so no need to draw both.
9 Mark relevant measurements on your diagram. Divide the bust and ease measurement by two for front and back and mark on your diagram across the full width, e.g., 92 ÷ 2 = 46 cm (36 ÷ 2 = 18″)
10 Convert measurements into stitches and rows.

N.B. At this point you must decide whether to use metric or imperial measurements throughout, as comparative measurements are not always exact equivalents and may cause unnecessary confusion. We will continue in centimetres for stitch calculations.

Tension = 20 sts per 10 cm
$$= \frac{20}{10} = 2 \text{ sts per cm}$$

74 Rectangular sweaters by (upper left) Vidhya Lockyer, (right) Maureen O'Dwyer, (lower left) Janet Thompson, unfinished sweater by Carole Fisher

First multiply the stitches per cm by the width measurements required. So front width measurement of 46 cm = 46 × 2 sts = 92 sts.

Add one stitch at each end of row for seam allowances, e.g., 92 + 2 sts = 94 sts.

This will be the number of stitches you cast on for a straight up and down style without a clinging welt. Good stitches for edges which lie flat and do not curl up are garter and moss stitch.

Ribbed welts

Ribbed welts cling to the body and are usually knitted on needles two sizes smaller than the main body. Deduct 10 per cent of the stitches for a ribbed welt style which grips more firmly.

e.g., 94 sts − 9.2 = 84 sts

Decide how deep the welt should be and mark your diagram, e.g., 5 cm.

To bring you back to your original stitch numbers after completing the welt, increase in every 9th stitch across the last rib row, or the first row of the main body of the knitting. Mark the diagram. Any stitches left over are split between the beginning and end of the row.

Now convert your vertical measurements into row numbers:

If your tension is 38 rows per 10 cm then your welt will be

$$\frac{38}{10} \times 5 \text{ rows deep} = \frac{190}{10} = 19 \text{ rows}$$

N.B. You should really knit a separate ribbing swatch on smaller needles for an accurate conversion here, but we won't complicate matters at this stage. Deduct the welt depth from your finished garment length and add a further 5 cm for a matching ribbed section across the top edge. This will give a suitable finished edge for a slash neckline, e.g., 50 − (5 + 5) = 40 cm length

Now multiply your row tension by the remaining body length measurement

$$\frac{38 \times 40 = 152 \text{ rows}}{10}$$

Mark on your neck width and armhole depth measurements.

Convert armhole measurements into stitches per cm to be picked up sideways around opening. Remember that both back and front of armhole openings need to be included. So multiply armhole depth (back and front) by stitch tension,

$$\text{e.g., } \frac{20}{10} \times 40 \text{ cm} = 80 \text{ stitches}$$

75 Measurement diagram for example A and B

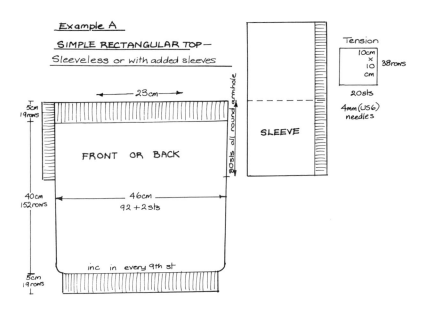

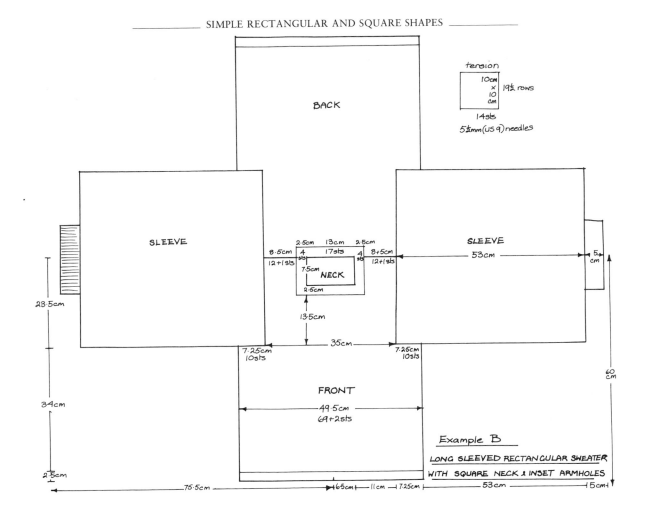

75 *Diagram B*

Decide depth of armhole ribbing, e.g., 2.5 cm,

e.g., $\dfrac{38}{10} \times 2.5 = 9\frac{1}{2}$ rows

Round number of rows up or down to nearest whole number and mark on diagram.

Using diagrams

All the instructions needed to knit this design are now included on the diagram. A brief visual pattern format similar to this is used successfully in Japanese hand-knitting patterns, enabling knitters to see at a glance how shapes are constructed. Pages of written instructions are unnecessary when you know how to interpret a diagrammatic pattern, and you also develop the knowledge and confidence to tackle your own design and fitting variations with ease. Unfortunately, this system is not as widely adopted as it should be since it unlocks the secrets of pattern shaping for all handknitters, not just designers and machine knitters as at present.

76 *Labelled tension swatch for example B*

Row by row instructions

Until you become more familiar with the use of diagrams and charted patterns you may find it helpful to add your own row by row instructions too, using the plan to guide you. Start at your intended cast on edge and work across the diagram, converting the information into row by row instructions in logical knitting order. For example:
Back and front
With size 3 mm (US 2) needles cast on 84 sts and work in K1, P1 rib for 18 rows (5 cm/2″) (19 rows including cast on row).
Next row Inc in 2nd and every foll 9th st (94 sts).
Change to size 4 mm (US 6) needles.
Work in g st for 152 rows (40 cm (16″))
Using smaller needles if necessary, change to K1, P1 rib for 18 rows (5 cm (2″)). Cast off in rib.
Making up
Sew up shoulder and side seams, leaving 20 cm (8″) openings for armholes amd 23 cm (9″) opening for neckline.
    Using 3 mm (US 2) needles, pick up 80 sts around armhole openings and work in K1, P1 rib for 9 rows.
    Cast off in rib.

Sleeved version
If you want to insert straight sleeves into these armholes, simply cast on 80 sts with the 3 mm needles as for armhole rib pick up and work cuff welt to depth required, or for fitted cuff cast on 40 sts and increase in every st across last row of rib.

Change to size 4 mm (US 3) needles and work in garter stitch to length required. Cast off and stitch into armholes. Alternatively, you could pick up 80 stitches around armhole and work *downwards* instead, reversing all instructions. This makes a stretchier armhole and saves the bother of sewing up the armhole seam. It also gives you the option of altering the sleeve length later if necessary.

Estimating your yarn requirements
If one ball knitted up produces an area of
18×46 cm $= 828$ sq.cm,
total area of front or back is 50×46 cm $= 2300$ sq.cm.
Double this figure for both pieces
(+ sleeves if included) $= 4600$ sq.cm.
Divide by the area knitted up in 1 ball
$$= \frac{4600}{828} = 5.55 \text{ balls}$$

$= 6$ balls $+1$ for margin of safety i.e. 7 balls altogether
(see page 98 for further details.)

EXAMPLE B

Steps 1, 2 and 3 The tension swatch for this design was knitted on size $5\frac{1}{2}$ mm (US 9) needles, using six different chunky weight fancy summer yarns and simple stitch variations of knit and purl, slipstitch and dropstitch.
4 The stitch and row tension over 10 cm (4″) varies slightly throughout the sample because of the differing yarns and stitches used, so measure it in several different places to even out any discrepancies and arrive at an average tension for use in your calculations.

e.g., *Stitch tension*

$$\frac{13 + 14.5 + 14 + 15}{4}$$
sts per 10 cm (4″)

$$= \frac{56}{4} = 14.125 \text{ for av}$$
No. of sts per 10 cm

$- 14$ sts per 10 cm
(to nearest $\frac{1}{2}$ st)

Row tension

$$\frac{18\frac{1}{2} + 19\frac{1}{2} + 20}{3}$$
rows per 10 cm (4″)

$$= \frac{58}{3} = 19.333$$
av rows

$= 19\frac{1}{2}$ rows per 10 cm

77 Square cushions using texture and pattern

5 Make a rough sketch of your intended design.
6 Take body measurements.
7 Add appropriate ease allowances (see chart p96). This example is intended to be a fairly loose fitting sweater so 8 cm (3″) has been added to bust measurement and 25% to wrist and armhole sizes.

Body measurements
e.g. Bust = 91 + 8 = 99 cm (36 + 3 = 39″)
Finished garment length = 60 cm (23½″)
Armhole depth = 19 + 4.7 = say 23.5 cm
$(7\frac{1}{2} + 1\frac{7}{8} = 9\frac{3}{8}″)$
Shoulder to shoulder = 35 cm (13¾″)
Neck to wrist = 75.5 cm (29¾″)
Wrist = 15 + 3.7 = say 18.5 cm
$(6 + 1\frac{1}{2} = 7\frac{1}{4}″)$
Front neck depth = 7.5 cm (3″)
Back neck width = 13 cm (5″)

8 Now draw a plan of the pattern pieces and add the appropriate measurements required. The plan should show exactly how your design is shaped and

78 Patchwork sweater designed and knitted by Frieda Oxenham

constructed. This sweater will be knitted in four sections. The back and front are the same except for the neck, and the sleeves match each other exactly, so you only really need to mark one of each with the dimensions from your calculations. The armholes are indented slightly to give a more natural shoulderline.

Divide bust and ease measurement by 2 for front and back body width,

e.g., $\dfrac{99}{2}$ = 49.5 cm

9 Now calculate the other measurements you need.

Horizontal measurements

e.g., Body width − shoulder to shoulder = underarm cast off: 49.5 cm − 35 cm = 14.5 cm
Divide by 2 for each underarm:
14.5 ÷ 2 = 7.25 cm.

Shoulder to shoulder − neck width = left and right shoulder: 35 − 13 = 22 cm
Divide by 2 for each shoulder: 22 ÷ 2 = 11 cm
Deduct 2.5 cm for garter stitch border:
11 − 2.5 = 8.5 cm

Vertical measurements

e.g., Finished garment length − armhole depth = lower edge to underarm: 60 − 23.5 = 36.5 cm
Deduct 2.5 cm for garter stitch border:
36.5 − 2.5 = 34 cm
Armhole depth − front neck depth = underarm to front neckline: 23.5 − 7.5 = 16 cm
Deduct 2.5 cm for garter stitch border:
16 − 2.5 = 13.5 cm
Neck to wrist less half shoulder to shoulder = sleeve length: 75.5 − 17.5 = 58 cm
Deduct a further 5 cm for a ribbed cuff:
58 − 5 = 53 cm
So main body of sleeve = 53 cm

10 Convert all measurements into stitches and rows as before. Some vertical measurements will not need conversion. See written instructions below *. This style has a 2.5 cm (1″) garter stitch border at the lower edge and around the square neckline so you do not have to enlarge the neck opening to allow for a neckband to be added later.

11 and 12 Add seam allowances and estimate yarn requirements as before.

Write out row by row instructions.
Front body section only is shown here. Using main yarn A, cast on 71 sts with size $5\frac{1}{2}$ mm (US 9) needles and work in g st for 2.5 cm (1″).

Change to yarn B and work first stitch pattern from swatch, changing yarns and stitch patterns as required and working straight until armhole level is reached (* 36.5 cm from beg.—no need for row calculation.)

Cast off 10 sts at beg of next 2 rows (51 sts).
Work straight in patt for 13.5 cm ($5\frac{1}{2}$″).
Next row Work 13 sts in patt. K25 sts for g st neckline border in main col, ending with 13 sts in patt.

Cont in patt and border as set for 2.5 cm (1″).
Next row Work 13 sts in patt. K4 sts main col, cast off 17 sts, K4 sts main col, work 13 sts in patt.
Work each shoulder separately, keeping 4 sts at neck edge in g st with main col, and rem sts in patt until work measures $23\frac{1}{2}$ cm ($8\frac{1}{2}$″) from armhole.
Cast off.

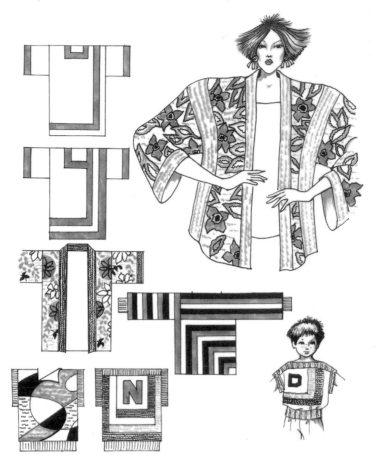

79 Ideas for rectangular and T-shaped garments

Making up

Join shoulder seams.

Sleeves are knitted separately and stitched into the armholes with the work laid out flat as shown in the diagram.

Or pick up sleeve head sts along F and B armhole edge and work downwards, knitting together one stitch from each end of the row on the needle with a stitch picked up from F & B underarm.

Cast off.

Remember to make allowances for different stitch and row tension at the joins so that work lies flat. For example if tension is 14 sts and $19\frac{1}{2}$ rows to 10 cm, pick up only 14 underarm sts for every $19\frac{1}{2}$ rows knitted.

Use these examples in whatever way you wish: copy the same shapes and dimensions substituting the tension from your chosen swatch; adapt the sizing to suit your own measurements, or simply use them as a general guide to basic shaping methods. Work out T shapes in the same way, casting extra blocks of stitches on and off for sleeves where required. Ideas for small knitting projects using squares are shown in fig. 80. They look equally effective when used in basic garment shapes such as those shown here, as do freeform pictures of the type used experimentally in Chapter 13 when sized up to a much larger scale. Here are some more simple garment shapes and ideas for possible development. Match them up to one of your own tension swatches and work out the details for yourself, or use them as a starting point for your own ideas. It doesn't matter if you can't draw— anyone can draw a basic rectangle! So scribble down a few basic shapes and play around with them to see what you come up with. Then work out your dimensions and convert them into your chosen swatch tension.

NEW WAYS OF LOOKING AT SQUARES

Here are some simple, small projects to build up your confidence. Use the squares joined together to make cushions, bags, shawls, slipovers, etc. For all squares the size required must be calculated first and then the tension worked out. Use the tension sample or yarn band if accuracy is not vital. For example, if the tension is 15 stitches per 10 cm/" (4"), cast on 60 stitches for one side of a 40 cm (16") square. Try any of the following:

Square one—colour strips

1 Work straight in col A for 4 cm (1½").
2 Next row, RS, work across row for 4 cm. Join on col B and work to end of row. Continue in A and B, as set for 4 cm.
3 Next row, RS, work across col A stitches, then same No. of col B sts. Join on col C and work to end of row. Cont in A, B and C as set for 4 cm.
4 Join on extra col every 4 cm until square is complete. Cast off.

Square two—diagonal square

1 Cast on 3 stitches. Inc 1 st at both ends of RS rows until 2 sides of square are completed.
2 Dec 1 st at both end of RS rows until 3 sts rem. Cast off.

Square three—three directions

1 Cast on sts for three sides of square plus 2 sts.
2 Divide sts into three groups with 1 marked st between each group.
3 Work to st before 1st marker, K3tog. Cont to st before 2nd marker, sk2po. Work to end of row. P next and every alternate row.
4 Rep these 2 rows until ½ original st No. left.
5 Graft both sets of sts together.

Square four—patchwork

Work sections in a clockwise direction.

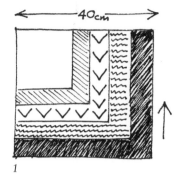

1

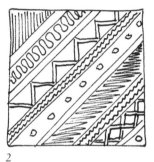

2

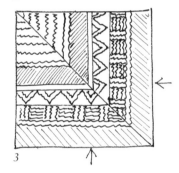

3

80 Simple squares

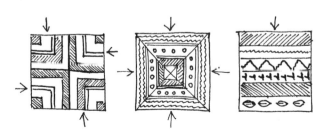

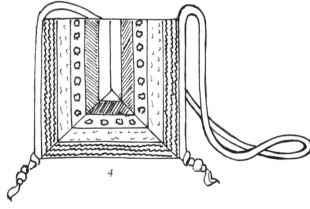

4

108

17
Ideas for edgings

Very few knitted fabric edges look acceptable on their own. Either they are not firm enough or they do not lie flat. The main exceptions are garter stitch, moss stitch and rib patterns—hence their frequent use. Ribbing has the added advantage of great elasticity which automatically adjusts to variations in size, stretching as needed, e.g., to pull over the head, and then returning to shape. Functional and/or decorative edging borders can either be worked at the same time as the main fabric (as in example A in Chapter 16); knitted in separate strips and attached later; or are added directly onto previously finished edges by picking up stitches and knitting on a border. The last two methods allow the designer to leave his or her options open for as long as possible before deciding what sort of edging will be most appropriate for a particular design. This may not be apparent until the design is at least partially made up and tested for fit. Edgings added at the last minute can also mean the difference between success and disaster for garments which turn out too large, since a baggy fit will look intentional if the cuffs and hem fit snugly, thereby stabilizing the garment. This allows the main body of the fabric to blouse attractively instead of hanging in a shapeless mess and swamping the wearer. Some cast off techniques also produce interesting edgings.

Picking up stitches
Generally speaking, for a firm, flat, yet elastic edge use needles 1–2 sizes smaller than those used for the main body of the knitting and pick up the correct number of stitches per cm or inch according to your own tension. With right side facing, insert the needle into the fabric one stitch in from the edge, winding the yarn around the point as if to knit, and drawing the loop through as many times as required. Be careful to enclose edges neatly and evenly and avoid leaving holes.

When designing your own garments or adapting pattern sizes you will need to calculate the correct number of stitches to be picked up around the edges. Measure the total distance required and multiply

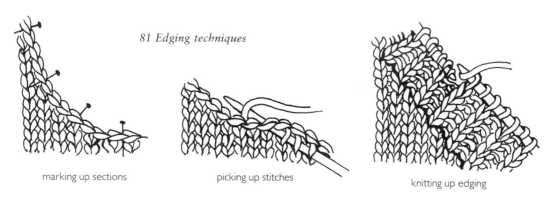

81 Edging techniques

marking up sections   picking up stitches   knitting up edging

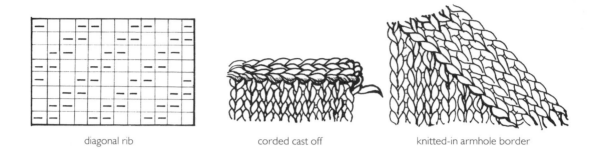

diagonal rib   corded cast off   knitted-in armhole border

this by the number of stitches per cm or inch from your edging tension sample. Or simply divide your edge into 2.5 cm or 1″ sections with marker pins and knit up the required number of stitches per section. This will also ensure even stitch distribution, for example, six stitches for every seven rows. Double check accuracy by knitting up a small section of edging only and seeing whether it lies correctly

before picking up all the way round. You can also try out alternative border patterns, colours, etc. in the same way to see what looks best before committing yourself. This can often save a great deal of wasted time later on.

Ribbed edge
These are the classic stitch choice for edgings,

82 Types of edgings: (from top left clockwise) *twisted rib, diagonal rib, stocking stitch hem, picot padded edging*

110

whatever method is used. Basic single and double rib is explained in detail on page 31, but you might like to try some of these variations too. Double knit fisherman's rib is worked by knitting in the stitch one row below on alternate stitches. Twisted rib involves working a knit stitch through the back loop with P1, P2 or P3 ribs,

e.g., (with multiple of 3 sts + 2):

Row 1 * P2, K1 tbl, rep from * to end, P2.
Row 2 K2, * P1 tbl, K2 rep from * to end.
Rep. these 2 rows for P2, K1 twisted rib.

Experiment with garter ribs (2 garter sts and 2 stocking sts) and ribs with cables interspersed too.

Diagonal ribbing counteracts any tendency for ribs to roll on sideways edges, e.g., cardigan openings, and is made by working a K2, P2 rib which moves 1 stitch sideways on each successive row. Alternatively, increase 1 stitch at the beginning of each RS row while decreasing 1 stitch at the end of the same row for an alternative diagonal effect.

Rolled edges

These make a feature of the fact that stocking stitch naturally curls at the edges.

With RS facing, pick up and knit in stocking stitch to the required depth (RS rows K, WS rows P).

Cast off.

The edge will roll up immediately showing the rev st st side uppermost. It needs no sewing down to stay in place.

Stocking stitch hems

With RS facing, pick up and knit a stocking stitch edge to required depth.

Purl 1 row on the RS. This forms a turning row.

Continue in st st for the same No. rows as before, then cast off.

Fold back along turning row and sew down the stitches to the base of the picked up row.

Picot hems

These are a variation of the above. The turning row forms a decorative edge, often used on babies' garments, but also suitable for a far wider range of design possibilities. (See colour section and opposite.) Work picot turning row as follows:

(K2tog, yf) rep to end of row, ending K1.

Next row P as normal.

A row of holes is formed which turn into picots when folded along picot row.

Can also be used on ridges.

83 Coat with rolled-edge sleeves and neck line. (Photo Raymond Palmer)

Tubular corded cast off edges

These look rather similar to rolled edges. Use a contrast colour for maximum effect and clarity. (MC = main colour; C = contrast colour.)

With RS facing at beg of cast off row, cast 3 sts *onto* LH needle with C. *K2 C, K2tog IMC + 1C.

Slip 3C stitches back onto L needle*.

Rep * to *.

You are casting off 1 st each time you knit 2 sts together. The 3 contrast sts are always ahead of the other stitches on LH needle and form a tubular knitted edge. Try out other decorative cast offs with the help of a stitch dictionary, e.g., cable, lacy and leaf edge cast offs.

Knitted-in borders

These need preplanning but enable you to knit and finish the garment and its borders in one operation, simply by changing stitch pattern near the edges. Try to use stitches which lie flat without blocking, for example, garter stitch and moss stitch, and keep to main body stitch tension where possible or you may need to work short rows where the patterns

84 Knitted-in mass stitch border

85 Pre-finished border

Prefinished border (as used on sleeveless cotton chevron sweater, colour plate 11)
Work a 4 stitch sl1, P1, sl1, P1 border as follows:
With yarn at back, (sl1 Pwise, yf, P1, yb) twice.
The sequence is always the same whether it is on the right or the wrong side of the work or at the beginning or end of the row, and produces a neatly rounded prefinished edge. This border can also be used to cast off horizontal edges such as underarm stitches in order to encircle armholes completely.
Work to armhole level, ending with RS row. With WS facing cast *on* 4 sts.
These will be used to cast *off* underarm sts by working to and fro as follows:
Slipping border sts Pwise as before *sl1, P1, sl1, P2tog (1 border st with 1 underarm st).
Turn, sl1, P1, sl1, P1 as above.
Turn *.
Rep from * to * casting off required No. of armhole sts.
Work WS row to end.
Cast on 4 sts.
Rep from * to *, casting off required sts at other underarm edge. Complete RS row to end, and work 1 more WS row, keeping first and last 4 stitches in sl1, P1, sl1, P1 border pattern. Now work as many armhole decs as required on RS rows (between main body and border pattern).

change so that the work lies flat, for example, working six border rows for every four rows of main pattern (see page 139). For neat sleeveless armholes or shaped edges work all shaping to the inside of the border stitches where they will not interfere with the border pattern. A ribbed border usually works well here, lying flat yet naturally following the curve required without twisting or wrinkling. Alternatively, try the following border that is sideways knitted at the underarm.

86 Ruffled edge

87 Sideways rib

88 Sleeveless peplum jacket with padded roll edges

Then continue straight to shoulder, still keeping border pattern correct.

Separate edging strips

These are usually knitted after the main fabric has been completed, and are worked in any direction on small numbers of stitches until the edging strip is long enough to fit the corresponding edge exactly. The two edges are then sewn together. Simple cardigans and jackets often have a separate narrow neck band which goes up one side of the front and down the other side, very often incorporating buttonholes. It is usually knitted vertically, starting with the buttonhole end so that the buttonholes can be spaced accurately, while the other end is adjusted to exactly the right length after pinning around the edges.

Fancy borders for shawls and skirts are often knitted sideways and there are dozens of glorious traditional lacy patterns to choose from. You can also introduce fullness with a frilled or ruffled edge.

Ruffled edge

(Worked sideways) Vary the stitch numbers to make wider or narrower bands.
Cast on 13 sts.
Row 1 Knit.
Row 2 P10, turn, looping yarn round next st thus: (yb, sl1, turn, yb, sl1) K10.
Row 3 P10, K3.
Row 4 K3, P10.
Row 5 K10 (yf, sl1, turn, yf, sl1) P10.
Row 6 Knit.
Rep Rows 1–6.

Sideways rib

If you dislike calculating how many stitches to cast on at the bottom of sweaters then this edging is the perfect answer.

Unlike most separate edging strips it is often knitted first rather than last. It strongly resembles a K3, P3 rib, yet is worked sideways until it forms a strip long enough to fit exactly around your body measurement at waist or hip level without any need for calculations whatsoever. Join the first and last row into a circle, then pick up stitches from the row ends and knit up vertically as normal for the body of your sweater, or attach by sewing if you have already worked the main body sections. (See fig. 100). This example is worked in two colours for clarity, but use one colour only if you prefer.
Col 1 Row 1 Knit.
Row 2 Knit.
Row 3 Purl.
Row 4 Knit.
Change to Col 2 Row 5 Knit.
Row 6 Purl.
Repeat rows 1–6 for length required.
Pick up 4 sts for every 6 rows along rib edge and continue vertically in st st.

Padded edgings

Last, but not least, you can make a striking feature of any double thickness edgings and hems by accentuating them with enclosed rolls of washable polyester wadding, piping cord, etc. This adds definition to edgings and can become quite a dominant design element in its own right (see fig. 88. You can also attach lengths of french knitting which may be stitched down to outer edges singly, or twisted and plaited together for extra impact.

Now see what ideas you can think up for yourself and try out a few practical experiments.

18
Simple fitted shapes

Most knitters think of shaping purely in terms of today's accepted classic sweater shape—a straight, easy fitting, hip length body shape, with set in armholes and long fitted sleeves. This basic shape has remained constant for almost three decades, except for variations in the amount of ease considered fashionable, and it has never ceased to amaze me that the much wider range of creative shapes possible for knitwear has been largely ignored for so long. But at last change is afoot now that finer yarns and fitted waistline knits reminiscent of the 50s and earlier are starting to be seen again. This opens up a wealth of new design shaping possibilities.

Of course, the demand for oversized garments in recent years also popularized very basic structural shapes like rectangles, T squares and batwings. New knitters loved these—and no wonder, because they demanded little technical skill or knowledge to knit up successfully. One size patterns knitted on large needles were quick and easy to work. Shoulders were dropped or non-existent, yet the results looked good, fitted anybody, and were marvellously comfortable to wear. This attracted a younger generation of largely self-taught knitters and designers, often with a design training and working background in other aspects of textiles like weaving, printed textiles or fashion. They cast aside many of the old rules and produced an explosion of exciting hand knitwear designs which relied for effect on texture and colour rather than shape.

This is still the best approach for newcomers because many knitters find that mental panic sets in at the mere mention of mathematical calculations. If you recognize yourself at this point, stick with rectangular shapes for a while (see chapter 16), or try some of the smaller projects to build up confidence before continuing. But different shapes are really not that difficult to master if you take them slowly one step at a time.

For those who are still with me, we're now moving onto the planning of simple fitted shapes. Classic, fitted sleeves and waisted body shapes with set in armholes are dealt with in exactly the same way up to the armhole. They are more appropriate for styles with a medium or tight fit because unlike rectangular styles with dropped armholes, the sleeves do not stick straight out from the body like a scarecrow, but form an angle of about 35 degrees with the horizontal at shoulder level, which improves the fit by reducing the surplus folds of fabric at the underarm when the arms are lowered. In comparison, the raglan sleeve should fall somewhere between these two, following the natural shoulder slope at an angle of roughly 15 degrees. It is therefore best suited to medium and loose fittings.

FITTED BODY SHAPE WITH SET IN SLEEVES (see page 116)

Body measurements required (No ease allowance included since example shown here is close fitting.)

Bust = 92 cm (36″)
Waist = 72 cm (28¼″)
Shoulder depth = 2 cm (¾″)
Armhole depth = 19 cm (7½″)
Back neck to waist = 42 cm (16½″)
Shoulder to shoulder = 35 cm (13¾″)
Back neck width = 13 cm (5″) } + neckband
Front neck depth = 7.5 cm (3″) } allowance

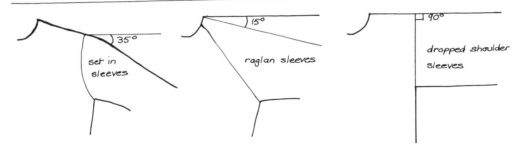

VARIABLE SLEEVE ANGLES WITH THE HORIZONTAL AT SHOULDER LEVEL

Shoulder length = 11.5 cm ($4\frac{1}{2}''$)
Neck to wrist = 75.5 cm ($29\frac{3}{4}''$)
Upper arm = 30 cm (12″)
Wrist = 16 cm ($6\frac{1}{4}''$)

Back

*Calculate half bust and waistline level stitch
numbers* as in Chapter 16, allowing for ease if
required. This example is close fitting so no ease is
included.

e.g., if tension measures 30 sts/38 rows to 10 cm
using 3 mm (US 2) needles and 4 ply yarn:

$$\frac{1}{2} \text{ bust} = 46 \times \frac{30}{10} = 138 \text{ sts}$$

$$+2 \text{ sts seam allowance} = 140 \text{ sts}$$

$$\frac{1}{2} \text{ waistline} = 36 \times \frac{30}{10} = 108 + 2 = 110 \text{ sts}$$

No. of sts to be increased between waist and
underarm level is: 140 − 110 = 30 sts
Divide this number into regular increases at either
end of row = 15 increase rows.

The waist to underarm seam (and corresponding
sleeve underarm) is difficult to measure accurately
on the body unless a skintight fit is required. So it is
wiser to calculate this measurement by deducting
the combined shoulder depth and armhole depth
from the total back neck to waist measurement,
e.g., 42 − (19 + 2) = 21 cm (not including the
ribbed edge which will extend below the waist).
Multiply this figure by the number of rows per 10
cm in your tension sample and divide by 10:

$$= 21 \times \frac{38}{10} = 79.8 = 80 \text{ rows}$$

The last 5 cm or so below the armhole should be
worked straight:

$$5 \times \frac{38}{10} = 19 \text{ rows approx}$$

Subtract this number from your total number of

rows: 80 − 19 = 61 rows
Divide 61 rows by 15 evenly-spread increase rows to
establish the frequency of the increases:

$$\frac{61}{15} = 4 \text{ remainder } 1 \text{ (r 1)}.$$

Add remainder to 19 straight rows = 20 rows
So after casting on 110 sts and completing the
required depth of ribbing (6 cm) at waistline on size
$2\frac{1}{4}$ mm (US 1) needles, change to size 3 mm (US 2)
needles and increase at both ends of every 4th row
15 times until there are 140 sts.
Work straight for 20 rows to armhole.

Armhole

Subtract shoulder to shoulder from half bust
measure for No. of sts to be decreased, e.g.,
140 − 107 sts = 33 sts (32 sts to give even No.).
Divide into 4, cast off one quarter at beg of next 2
rows then dec 1 st at both ends of every alt row until
only shoulder sts remain (108 sts).
i.e., cast off 8 sts at beg of first 2 rows, then 1 st at
both ends of foll 8 alt rows.
Cont straight until armhole depth measurement
is complete (19 cm).

Shoulders

Measure required finished back neck width
(av neck width 13 cm) and add allowance each
side for neck band width, e.g., (2 + 13 + 2) cm =
17 cm = 51 sts (say 52 sts to give even No.).
Subtract total back neck width from shoulder sts,
e.g., 108 − 52 = 56 sts
Divide by 2 for each shoulder = 28 sts
Cast off these sts gradually over next few rows
according to shoulder depth, e.g., 6 rows.
Divide each shoulder into 3, e.g., 10, 9, 9, sts
Cast off each group of sts at beg of next 6 rows.
The remaining back neck sts can either be cast off or
left on a stitch holder until neckband is worked.

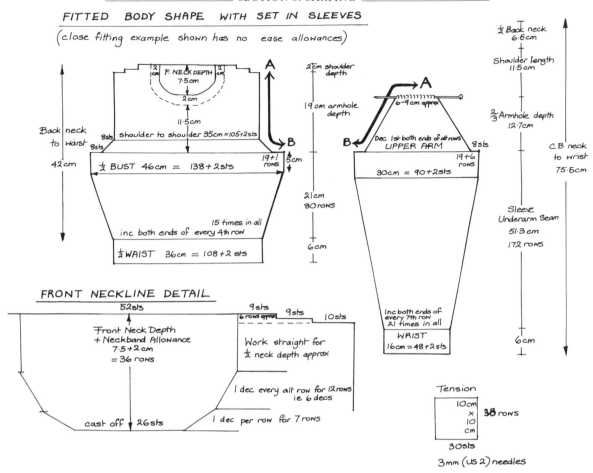

FITTED BODY SHAPE WITH SET IN SLEEVES

(close fitting example shown has no ease allowances)

F. NECK DEPTH 7·5cm

2cm | 2cm

2cm

A

11·5cm

8sts shoulder to shoulder 35cm =105+2sts

8sts

B

Back neck to waist 42cm

½ BUST 46cm = 138+2sts

19+1 rows 5cm

15 times in all inc both ends of every 4th row

½ WAIST 36cm = 108+2 sts

2cm shoulder depth

19 cm armhole depth

A

6-9cm approx

B

Dec 1st both ends of alt rows UPPER ARM

8sts

19+6 rows

30cm = 90+2sts

Inc both ends of every 7th row 21 times in all

WRIST 16cm = 48+2sts

21cm 80 rows

6cm

½ Back neck 6·5cm

Shoulder length 11·5cm

⅔ Armhole depth 12·7cm

C B neck to wrist 75·5cm

Sleeve Underarm Seam 51·3cm 172 rows

6cm

FRONT NECKLINE DETAIL

52sts

Front Neck Depth + Neckband Allowance 7·5+2 cm = 36 rows

9sts

9sts

6 rows approx

10sts

Work straight for ½ neck depth approx

1 dec every alt row for 12 rows ie 6 decs

cast off 26sts

1 dec per row for 7 rows

Tension

10cm × 10 cm

38 rows

30sts

3mm (US 2) needles

89 Planning fitted shapes

Front
Work as for back until beginning of neckline shaping.

Neckline
Find this position by adding armhole depth (19 cm) to shoulder depth (2 cm) and subtracting front neck depth (7.5 cm) + neckband allowance (2 cm):
21 − (7.5 + 2) = 11.5 cm
i.e., work as for back until front measures 11.5 cm from beginning of armhole shaping.
Front neckline width at shoulder = finished back neck width (52 sts).

Cast off roughly half these sts immediately at centre front (26 sts).
Then dec rem sts over roughly half of available neck depth rows,
e.g., neck depth (7.5 cm) + neckband depth (2 cm) = 9.5 cm.

$$= 9.5 \times \frac{38}{10} = 36 \text{ rows} \qquad \frac{36}{2} = 18 \text{ rows}$$

So dec 26 sts over 18 rows approx.
Decrease quickly at first, then more slowly, working each side of neckline separately, e.g., Dec 13 sts each side of neckline, working 1 dec per row for 7 rows.

Then 1 dec every alt row for 12 rows (6 decs). Total 19 rows.

Front shoulder sts should now match back shoulders (28 sts).

Work straight until armhole measure is completed.

Shoulders

Shape shoulders as for back, casting off sts in groups as before, but on alt rows only.

Sleeves

Work out sleeve shaping up to armhole level as for back. The sleeve underarm seam measure is calculated by subtracting the combined shoulder length and average sleeve cap depth from the total neck to wrist measurement (the average sleeve cap depth) is two thirds of armhole depth (approx)), e.g.,

Sleeve cap depth $= \frac{2}{3} \times 19 = 12.7$

Shoulder + sleeve cap $= 11.5 + 12.7$
$$= 24.2$$

Subtract from total neck to wrist measure $= 75.5 - 24.2 = 51.3$ cm

Also subtract the depth of ribbed cuff unless it is to be worn turned back.

$51.3 - 6 = 45.3$ cm

Convert sleeve underarm seam, upper arm and wrist measurements into stitches or rows as before, using tension per 10 cm from your sample.

Sleeve underarm seam $= 45.3 \times \frac{38}{10} = 172.1$

$$= 172 \text{ rows}$$

Upper arm $= 30 \times \frac{30}{10} = 90 + 2$ st seam allowance
$$= 92 \text{ sts}$$

(add ease if close fit not required on sleeve)

Wrist $= 16 \times \frac{30}{10} = 48 + 2$ sts $= 50$ sts

Divide the difference into regular increases between wrist and underarm, e.g.,

$92 - 50 = 42$ increase sts

$\frac{42}{2}$ (both ends of row) $= 21$ increase rows

Last 5 cm below armhole to be worked straight as on back (19 rows), i.e., 21 increase rows to be spread evenly over $172 - 19$ rows $= 153$ rows.

Frequency of increases $= \frac{153}{21} = 7r6$

Add remainder to 19 straight rows $= 25$ rows.

So after casting on 50 sts and working 6 cm of ribbing, increase at both ends of every 7th row 21 times until there are 92 sts.

Work straight for 25 rows to armhole.

Sleeve cap (simplified method)

Work as for back armholes, e.g., Cast off 8 sts at beg of next 2 rows, then dec 1st at both ends of every alt row.

Cont decs until half the sleeve cap edge including half the sts still on needle equals armhole edge measurement of body. (See lines AB on fig. 89).

Row width on needle should be 6–9 cm approx $= 16$–27 sts.

Cast off straight.

PLANNING SHAPES ON KNITTERS' GRAPH PAPER

I have shown the above sleeve cap shaping method because it is by far the simplest to use and gives good results. Conventional curved sleeve caps are notoriously difficult to plan successfully, but if you wish to try, take a sheet of knitters' graph paper in the correct tension grid for your design and plot out various experimental curved sleeve caps, using the following guidelines to help you produce an accurate result.

Mark out the upper arm stitch width, using one square per stitch. The cast off stitches for the first two rows and first few rows of armhole shaping should match those cast off on the body. The usual sleeve cap depth is roughly two thirds of the armhole depth, and the sleeve top cast off edge should measure 5 cm (2″) approx, or you can work out the precise number of rows in the sleeve cap as follows.

No of sleeve cap rows = armhole depth less $\frac{1}{2}$ sleeve top cast off, less 2 cm (on all sizes) for a good fit over shoulder,

e.g., $19 - 2.5 - = 14.5$ cm

Convert into rows $= 14.5 \times \frac{38}{10} = 55$ rows
$$= 54 \text{ (even No. needed)}$$

Subtract sleeve top and underarm cast off sts on body from sleeve undearm sts,

e.g., $92 - (5 \times \frac{30}{10}) + (2 \times 8)$ sts

$92 - (15 + 16)$

$92 - 31 = 61$ more sts to be decreased gradually over sleeve cap

$= 30$ sts each side (even No. needed)

Mark in sleeve top cast off row centrally, 15 sts wide and 54 rows above underarm. As a general rule of thumb, begin plotting armhole curve downwards from top, dec 1 st on every row, also working upwards from armhole dec 1 st on alt rows until curves meet. Experiment until you produce a gentle overall curve with a pleasing, rounded top.

ALTERNATIVE NECKLINES

You can easily work out any neckline shape you choose with the help of knitters' graph paper. There is no need when planning simple slash, square and boat shapes without curves and diagonals, since small measurement diagrams are quite adequate for these. But it is extremely useful when planning anything more complex, since you can draw out your intended shape and see exactly how areas requiring greater definition will look in proportion to the rest of the garment. For example, it is usual to begin the shaping of classic V necklines at the same time as the armhole shaping, but there is absolutely no reason why you should not make them much shallower or deeper if you prefer. You may also wish to include fancy cut out shapes such as key hole necklines, or plan multi-coloured neckline border patterns or front placket openings etc.

I have outlined only a few of the basic shaping methods here as there are already several excellent books on the market which deal with standard knitwear shaping methods, such as, *Knitting Your Own Designs For A Perfect Fit* by Montse Stanley, *The Knit Kit*, and *Knitting by Design* by Mary Anne Erickson and Eve Cohen (See booklist at the back of book).

Now let's start thinking about very different approaches to shaping.

Pattern Project 7 ✖ ✖ ✖

Fitted silk sweater with diamond eyelet pattern, gathered elbow-length sleeves and pointed welts

See colour section

Measurements

To fit size 81 (86, 91, 97) cm/32 (34, 36, 38)″ bust. Actual measurements: bust, 81 (86, 91, 97) cm/32 (34, 36, 38)″; waist, 61 (66, 71, 76) cm/24 (26, 28, 30)″.

Finished length from top of shoulder to waist 41 (41.5, 42.5, 43) cm/16$\frac{1}{4}$ (16$\frac{1}{2}$, 16$\frac{3}{4}$, 17)″.

Pointed welt depth from waist 21.5 (23, 24.5, 26) cm/8$\frac{1}{2}$, 9, 9$\frac{1}{2}$, 10″. (Shallow version 13 (14, 15, 15.5) cm/5 (5$\frac{1}{2}$, 6, 6$\frac{1}{4}$)″.

Sleeve underarm to lower edge of cuff at side seam 23 cm/9″.

(knitting kits also available, see page 155)

Materials

135 (150, 165, 180) g fine pure silk in main col (MC). 65 (70, 75, 80) g tussah silk in contrast col (C). 1 pair size 2$\frac{3}{4}$ mm (US 2) needles throughout.

Tension

36 sts and 44 rows to 10 cm (4″) over patt in fine silk (wash sample before checking tension). 44 sts and 40 rows to 10 cm (4″) over rib in tussah silk.

Abbreviations See page 10.

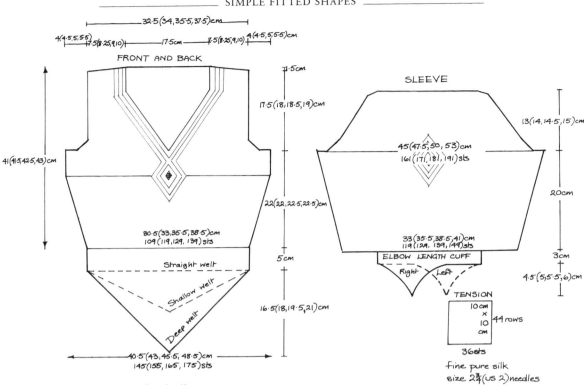

90 *Measurement diagram—fitted silk sweater*

Pattern
Project
7

NOTE When working from chart, read RS rows from R to L and WS rows from L to R, foll stitch diagram on chart for pattern.

BACK

Pointed welt versions

With C, cast on 3 sts, using cable method (see page 26).

Work in K1, P1 rib, casting on 2 sts at beg of each row to 133 (145, 157, 169) sts; or 4 sts to 131 (143, 155, 167) sts and 1 st both ends of last row if shallower welt is required.

Straight welt version Cast on full No. of sts.

All versions Then work straight in rib for 20 rows.

Change to MC and work *dec* rows as follows:

K8 (9, 10, 11), *K2tog, K3* 24 (26, 28, 30) times.

K5 (6, 7, 8). 109 (119, 129, 139) sts.

Work 1 (1, 3, 3) rows st st.

Omitting bobbles and diamond patt and cont eyelets as set throughout back, start working from chart at row 5 with a K-row.

Inc 1 st at both ends of this and every foll 4th row,

18 times in all. 145 (155, 165, 175) sts.

Cont straight until row 98 of chart has been completed. 96 (96, 98, 98) rows.

Armhole

Cast off 7 (8, 9, 10) sts at beg of next 2 rows 131 (139, 147, 155) sts

Then dec 1 st at both ends of next 5 (6, 7, 8) rows and foll 2 alt rows 117 (123, 129, 135) sts.

Work straight until 78 (80, 82, 84) rows from armhole have been completed.

Shoulder shaping

Cast off 9 (10, 11, 12) sts at beg of next 6 rows. Cast off rem 63 sts for B neck.

FRONT

Work as for back but incl. bobbles and starting large diamond patt at row 49 of chart as foll:

Inc in 1st st, K65 (70, 75, 80), yf, K2tog, K to last st, inc. (133 sts)

Row 50 Purl.

119

Row 51 K64 (69, 74, 79) skpo, yf, K1, yf, K2tog, K to end. Cont working from chart to armhole.

Armhole and front neck

Next row RS. Cast off 7 (8, 9, 10) sts & work to end of row.

Next row Cast off 7 (8, 9, 10) sts, work 65 (69, 73, 77) sts, dec 1, work to end.

Complete L side of neck first. Dec 1 st at armhole edge of next 5 (6, 7, 8) rows & foll 2 alt rows, also dec 1 st at neck edge on every alt row.

Keeping armhole edge straight, cont dec on every alt neck edge row until 27 (30, 33, 36) sts rem. Work straight for 14 (16, 18, 20) rows.

Shoulder shaping

Cast off 9 (10, 11, 12) sts at beg of next and foll 2 alt rows.

RS facing, rejoin yarn to rem sts and work as for L side of neck.

Work 1 more row before shoulder shaping.

RIGHT SLEEVE

With C, cast on 3 sts and work in K1, P1 rib, casting on 2 sts at beg of every row until there are 39 (43, 47, 51) sts.

Cast on 21 (22, 23, 24) sts at beg of next row. 60 (65, 70, 75) sts.

Work straight in rib for 3 cm (1¼″), ending with a WS row.

With MC work inc row, K1, inc in every st to end of row. 119 (129, 139, 149) sts.

Work 3 rows st st.

Start working patt from chart at row 5 with a K row, inc 1 st at both ends of this and every foll 4th row, 21 times in all. 161 (171, 181, 191) sts.

Cont straight until row 88 of chart has been completed.

Sleeve cap

Cast off 7 (8, 9, 10) sts at beg of next 2 rows.

Dec 1 st at both ends of next 7 (8, 9, 10) rows and foll 21 (22, 23, 24) alt rows.

Cast off 4 sts at beg of next 6 rows. Cast off rem 67 (71, 75, 79) sts.

(If you wish, pre-gather sleevehead by working K2tog across last row while casting off.)

Left sleeve

As for R sleeve, but reverse position of point on cuff by working 1 extra row before casting on 21 (22, 23, 24) sts.

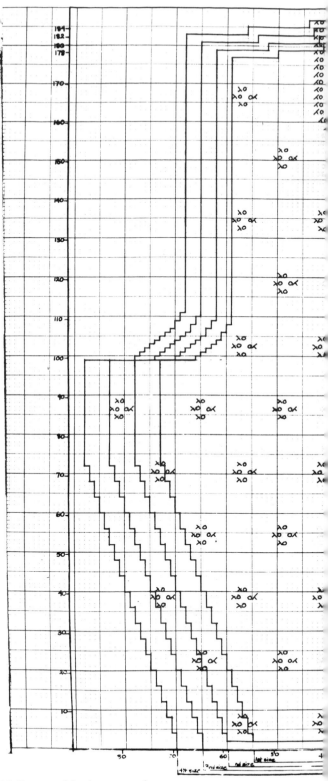

91 Front and back pattern chart

FITTED SILK SWEATER WITH DIAMOND EYELETS
BACK AND FRONT

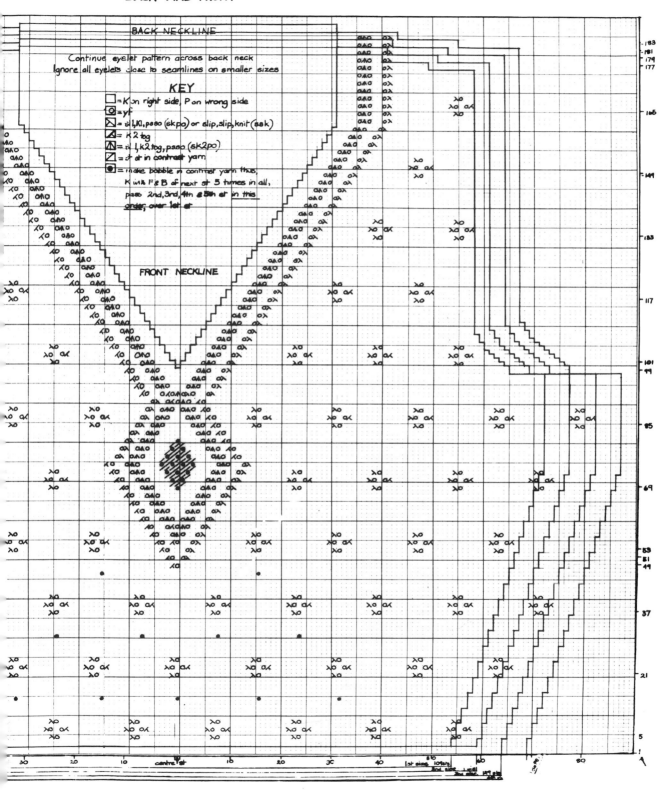

BACK NECKLINE

Continue eyelet pattern across back neck
Ignore all eyelets close to seamlines on smaller sizes

KEY

☐ = K on right side, P on wrong side
◉ = yf
◪ = sl 1, K1, psso (skpo) or slip, slip, knit (ssk)
◩ = K 2 tog
⟁ = sl 1, k 2 tog, psso (sk2po)
◿ = st st in contrast yarn
⬤ = make bobble in contrast yarn thus,
    K into F & B of next st 5 times in all,
    pass 2nd, 3rd, 4th & 5th st in this
    order, over 1st st

FRONT NECKLINE

centre st

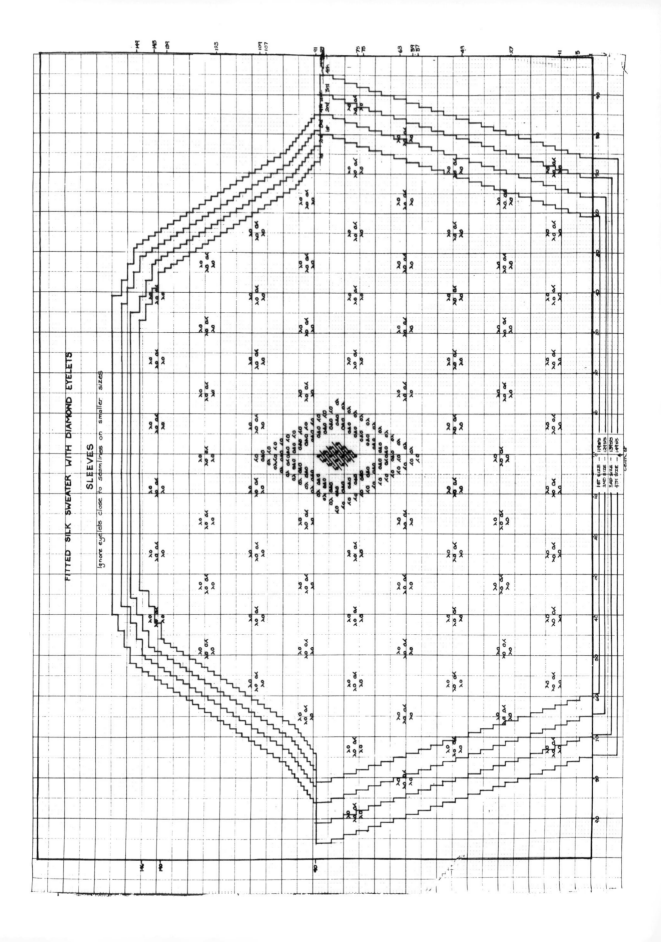

FITTED SILK SWEATER WITH DIAMOND EYELETS

SLEEVES

Ignore eyelets close to seamlines on smaller sizes

MAKING UP

Join R shoulder seam. With C, RS facing, pick up and K 48 (50, 52, 54) sts down L side of neck, 1 st at CF, (mark this st) 48 (50, 52, 54) sts up R side of neck and 62 sts across B neck. 159 (163, 167, 171) sts.

Row 1 (WS) Work in K1, P1 rib to within 2 sts of marked CF st, P2tog, P1, P2tog tbl rib to end.

Row 2 Rib to 2 sts before marker, K2tog tbl, K1, K2tog, rib to end. Rep these 2 rows 3 times more.

Cast off loosely in rib, still dec.

Join L shoulder and neckband.

Join side and sleeve seams. Sew sleeves into armholes, arranging gathers evenly over shoulder area for 10 cm (4″) approx.

Shoulder pads

With MC used double, cast on 3 sts.

Work in st st, inc both ends of RS rows until there are 41 sts.

Cast off loosely.

Roll up triangle to form shoulder pad and stitch to armhole inside sleeve head to pad out gathers.

Corded decoration

With MC used double, make 4 lengths of french knitted cord (see page 52). You will need 2 × 25 cm (2 × 10″) lengths, 2 × 20 cm (2 × 8″), and 2 longer ones to fit around armholes.

Stitch down longer lengths around armhole seams, placing join at shoulder.

Knot ends of shorter cord lengths, then pair one of each length together, knot in the middle and stitch to shoulder to cover join.

Thread in some knitting-in-elastic across B neck band to prevent stretching.

Pattern Project 7

92 Sleeve pattern chart

19
Knitting in all directions—more adventurous shapes

For most knitters the obvious direction in which to work is from the *bottom upwards*, simply because most knitting patterns are written that way. But what about knitting downwards, sideways or diagonally? Or how about working in two directions at once? When you start thinking about the design potential of all these alternatives, endless possibilities spring to mind. So let's consider a few of them and suggest how each may be used to advantage to produce stylish, well proportioned yet functional designs which use the unique shaping qualities of knitted fabric to maximum effect.

This last point is very important because many of the new breed of 'designer knitters' have been criticized for forcing their designs through the knitting process with scant regard for the finer points of shaping and finishing technique. This is hardly surprising when you consider that until the mid-70s at least, few art colleges offered design training in hand-knitted textiles. So most designers who later chose to express themselves through knitting had originally specialized in other aspects of art and design. Their knitting skills were largely self taught, but what they lacked in technical expertise they made up for in natural creative talent. Their solid design foundation enabled them to produce designs with an impact that catapulted knitting out of the doldrums and into the fashion limelight. It is ironic that even now, the knitters with the greatest pool of technical skill—that is, those who knitted long before the current knitting revival occured—tend to be those with the least confidence to design for themselves because they have copy knitted for so long that they feel totally lost without a pattern telling them what to do. If this sounds like you, here's your opportunity to shine!

93 Fitted shapes can be anything you make them. What could this be? Turn page upside down and new possibilities spring to mind. Creative thinkers experiment constantly by looking at things from a new angle. Try it for yourself.

124

Wild colours and textures may not be your cup of tea but when it comes to grasping the concepts of directional shaping your understanding should be streets ahead of most other knitters. And if you remember the complexities of knitted bust darts, keep a look out—they're on the way back too.

KNITTING FROM THE TOP

The main advantages are practical rather than visual with this method. Knitting downwards is particularly useful for children's garments which need to grow with them where possible. Sleeves can be picked up around the armholes and worked downwards, which not only gives a much stretchier armhole which is stronger and more comfortable in wear, but also allows for easy lengthening of the sleeves by unravelling at the lower edge, and adding longer cuffs or replacing worn elbow sections. Sweater, dress and skirt lengths can all be lengthened in the same way at the lower edge if the hem has been worked downwards rather than upwards. Don't worry if you cannot match the colour—add a contrast stripe or border pattern instead. Write out your pattern backwards, substituting decreases for increases and take care that any fancy stitch patterns won't look wrong if worked upside down. If they do, see if you can reverse them too.

Even a set-in sleeve cap can be picked up and

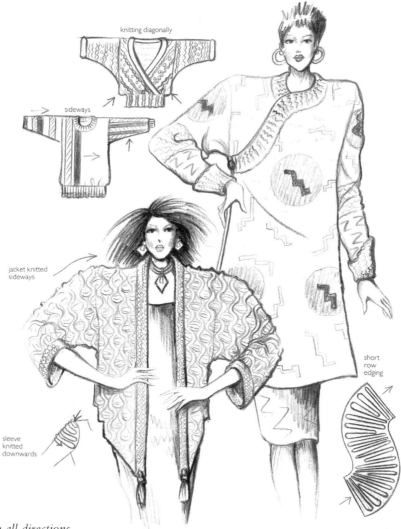

knitting diagonally

sideways

jacket knitted
sideways

sleeve
knitted
downwards

short
row
edging

94 Knitting in all directions

knitted downwards by reversing the usual pattern instructions. Using a circular needle, pick up and knit the correct numbers of cast off stitches across the shoulder section of the armhole. At the end of each row, gradually bring in however many stitches the pattern originally decreased or cast off, working to and fro until the entire armhole is on the needle at underarm level. Then work in rounds from underarm to cuff.

Another bonus is that if you prefer to design as you knit without planning ahead, it makes life much easier to get the neckline shaping out of the way first so you know exactly what space you have left before going to town with amazing, panoramic patterns. It also enables you to try on your garment and judge the correct body and sleeve length by looking at them rather than measuring in advance (see also page 146. Barbara Walker, one of the biggest names in American knitting, has devoted an entire book to this subject, *Knitting From The Top*.

KNITTING SIDEWAYS

No doubt you have noticed that batwing sweaters are often knitted sideways from cuff to cuff. Apart from the obvious practical advantage of having no armholes to worry about, one is struck by the fact that the stitch patterns on a sideways knitted body run vertically, so look very different on the sleeves where the same pattern is seen horizontally instead. How else can we use this to our advantage when designing? What about vertical stripes on a rectangular sleeveless top for example? These are always more flattering for fuller figures. Simply cast on sufficient stitches for the side seam instead of the lower edge and knit sideways across the full width of the fabric, changing colour as necessary for each new stripe until you reach the other side seam.

Vertical ridges can be worked in the same way, or try working sleeves sideways from one underarm seam to another, incorporating a bold central stripe or band of textured stitches. Remember to convert *vertical* measurements into stitches and *horizontal* measurements into rows when calculating for sideways knitted designs. There are practical advantages too—sideways knitted skirts seat far less, and front opening garments can be knitted in one piece, by casting off for the front opening and casting on again after working the neck shaping. This also makes it easier to pick up front edging bands horizontally, which tend to stretch less than those knitted vertically anyway.

KNITTING DIAGONALLY

Knit a simple square or rectangle diagonally and it immediately looks more interesting. Diagonal knits are always softly flattering to wear, whatever your shape or size. So how should you tackle diagonally-knitted rectangles?

Cast on three stitches at corner of lower edge. Increase regularly at both ends of row until one side seam is required length. Now begin decreasing at this end of row, also decreasing at other end when opposite seam reaches required half bust measurement. Continue decreasing until three stitches remain. Cast off. Any stripes or bands of pattern worked horizontally across the row will sit

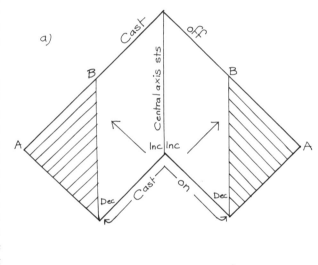

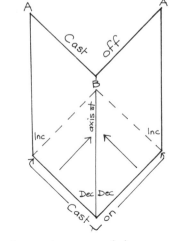

95 *Basic chevron increase and decrease method (with central axis st)*

diagonally on the finished garment. Diagonal knitting is very appropriate for wrapover garment styles since the front edges can be cast off straight and will hold their shape well.

CHEVRON KNITTING—INTEGRATED SHAPING WITHIN THE ROW

Now the fun really starts, because if you work increases in the middle of the row, counteracted by decreases at row ends, or vice versa, you can produce a multi-directional knitted fabric which lends itself to unusually inventive garment shapes which are easy fitting and infinitely adaptable. I call this way of working 'playing with shape' because this is exactly what one does, first on paper and then in yarn using the 'design as you knit' approach to keep your options open as long as possible and to avoid unnecessary calculations. Check the shape and fit of your work as you go along by holding your knitting up against you and checking both the outline shape and any interior shaping lines within the body of your garment before deciding what to do next.

First, cast on around 21 stitches and try knitting these two chevron shaping samples to help you grasp the basic concepts involved. They will help you to develop your ability to think constructively about shaping and will encourage you to experiment for yourself, since you will soon discover that the most obvious direction in which to knit is not always the most appropriate or visually effective. Think how you could use these concepts to create unusual designs of your own, then look at the pattern and project suggestions to help spark off some more ideas.

Basic chevron increase method (with central axis st) *(fig. 95a)*
Cast on an odd No. of sts. Mark centre st with coloured thread.

Row 1 K to centre st (axis) and inc 1 st on either side, then K to end of row.
Row 2 Purl.
A Rep these 2 rows to produce an ever-widening chevron shape.
B If you wish to keep the No. of sts constant, dec at both ends of K rows to counterbalance incs at centre.

Cast off. Use ml incs unless you wish to make a special feature of your chevron axis with pairs of open lacy, yf incs.

96 *Chevron knitted summer tops, designed and knitted by Frieda Oxenham*

Basic chevron decrease method (with central axis st) *(fig. 95b)*
Cast on as before.

Row 1 K to last 2 sts before central axis st, skpo, K1, K2tog, K to end of row.
Row 2 Purl.
A Rep these 2 rows, replacing dec sts with an inc at both ends of K rows if you wish to keep the st Nos constant.
B If you do not do this at your st Nos will gradually lessen until your knitting decreases to a point.
While knitting these two samples you will notice that your knitting hangs rather strangely on the needles, but will lie flat when you finally cast off, making angular shaped pieces of knitting with a point at either the cast on or cast off edge. Now look at Fig. 97 to see how these concepts have been used to create various knitted garments.

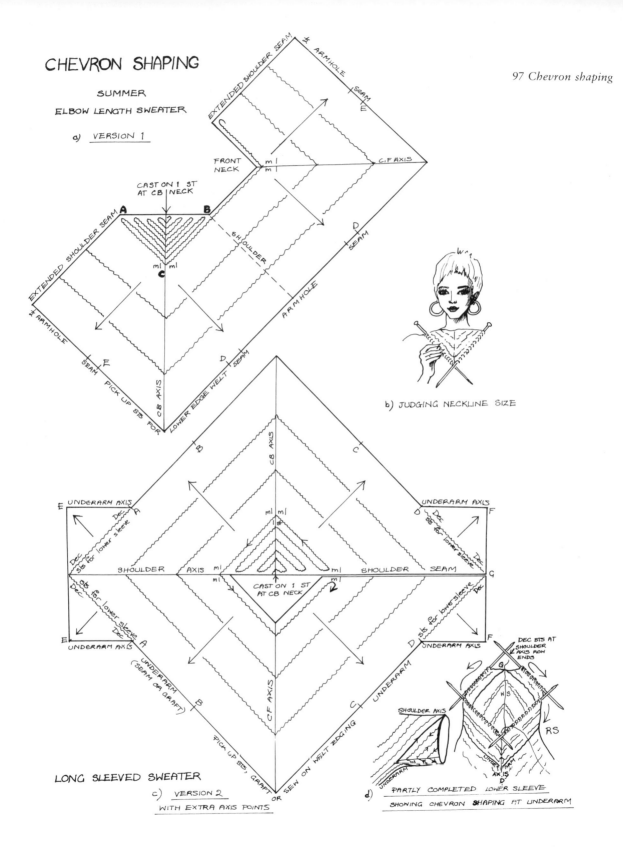

CHEVRON SHAPING

SUMMER
ELBOW LENGTH SWEATER

a) VERSION 1

EXTENDED SHOULDER SEAM

ARMHOLE SEAM

E

FRONT NECK

m l
m l

C.F AXIS

CAST ON 1 ST AT CB NECK

A   B

SHOULDER

D
SEAM

m l m l

C

ARMHOLE

EXTENDED SHOULDER SEAM

¼ ARMHOLE

SEAM

E

D

SEAM

PICK UP STS FOR

LOWER EDGE WELT

CB AXIS

b) JUDGING NECKLINE SIZE

B

CB AXIS

C

E   UNDERARM AXIS
A

Dec sts for lower sleeve

UNDERARM AXIS

D   F

Dec sts for lower sleeve

Dec

m l m l

SHOULDER   AXIS   m l

m l

SHOULDER   SEAM

G

Dec sts for lower sleeve

CAST ON 1 ST
AT CB NECK

2

Dec

E   A
UNDERARM AXIS

D   F
UNDERARM AXIS

Dec sts for lower sleeve

DEC STS AT SHOULDER AXIS FOR ENDS

UNDERARM (SEAM OR GRAFT)

B

CF AXIS

UNDERARM

C   UNDERARM

G

SHOULDER AXIS

RS

PICK UP STS, GRAFT

OR SEW ON WELT EDGING

UNDERARM AXIS

D

LONG SLEEVED SWEATER

c) VERSION 2
WITH EXTRA AXIS POINTS

d) PARTLY COMPLETED LOWER SLEEVE
SHOWING CHEVRON SHAPING AT UNDERARM

128

V neck

front and
back knitted
in one piece

shoulder

front

98 Using chevrons, working upwards: (top) directional
knitting design made by decreasing either side of the
central axis stitch; (bottom) design made by increasing
either side of the axis stitch.

Summer elbow-length sweater

(Figure 100)

Measurements

To fit bust 81–96 cm/32–38″.
Finished length from CB neck 69 cm/27″.

Materials

Assorted cotton and rayon summerweight yarns,
e.g., cotton perlé, ribbon, flammé, chenille, bias
strip.
Total weight approx 450 g.
$4\frac{1}{2}$ mm (US 7) circular needle—long. Set of double-
pointed needles size 4 mm (US 6) for rev st st and rib
and/or pair of $3\frac{1}{4}$ mm (US 3) for sideways rib.

*99 Measurement diagram—summer elbow length swea-
ter project*

Working method

Refer to fig. 97a for general working method
diagram. For details of sweater shown in fig. 100
follow the diagram below *(fig. 99)* and incorporate
your own stitch patterns.
No stitch calculations needed whatsoever!
Cast on 1 st at back neck, working downwards as
follows:
Inc in F & B of st. P every WS row. Mark central
axis st. Inc in first and last st and on either side of
axis st on K rows until ABC triangle shape *(fig. 97a)*
is same size as required F neck measurement.

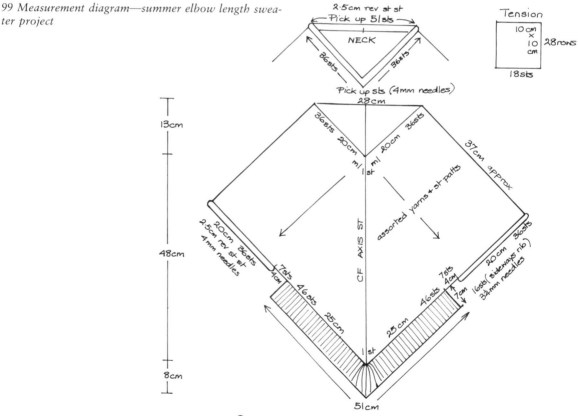

or For K1, P1 rib, using 4mm needles, pick up 184 sts + 1 axis st at CF+CB,
(186 sts all round) Inc each side of axis st on alt rounds for 7cm.

100 Summer elbow-length sweater (pattern project 8)

(K halfway across row to axis point and hold up work against neck to judge for size) *(fig. 97b)*.

K to end of row.

Count sts and cast on same amount again for front V neck, marking centre st for CF axis point.

P back along row, then work K row, inc either side of B & F axis sts (no more incs at beg and end of rows).

Cont until sweater is required length.

Cast off. Stitch shoulder seam.

Try on and pin side seams, leaving sufficient opening for armholes and chevron ribbed lower welt.

Pick up sts around openings and knit edgings as required.

This style may be knitted to and fro on circular needles with shoulder seam if you wish to use mixed colours, yarns or stitch patterns, so avoiding a step in pattern at beginning of round. Shoulder seam may be eliminated and knitting worked in the round if one yarn only is used. An alternative is to add axis points at shoulder and underarm for long sleeves. (See fig. 97c and pattern project 10.)

Now how about trying out a few ideas of your own using these chevron shaping techniques? Zigzags can also be made by knitting a repeating chevron sequence which is used on allover patterns or for decorative edgings at the bottom of jackets, sleeves and skirts.

101 Sleeveless top and other ideas for possible
development

132

Pattern Project 9

Knitted bags with chevrons, stripes, bobbles or picot edgings

102 Chevron knitted bags and variations. Clockwise from the top: small red and black bag in cotton linen; large purple and green bag in chunky cotton chenille; medium turquoise bag in chunky viscose tubular ribbon; two picot-edged bags in thick silk and wool.

BASIC STRIPED CHEVRON KNITTED BAG

This pattern can be knitted in any yarn or combinations of yarns, and is perfect for using up oddments of any colours you have available. Keep to approx similar yarn thickness throughout, or use doubled finer yarns if mixing yarn weights.

Measurements

This bag can be knitted to any length by adjusting the number of rows; its width will vary slightly according to yarns and needle sizes used (see examples for guidance). Small red/black bag in DK cotton/linen ③, 20 × 14 cm (8 × 5½″) approx, using 4½ mm (US 7) needles.

Medium turquoise bag in chunky viscose tubular ribbon ★★ 26 × 15 cm (10 × 6″) approx, using 6 mm (US 10) needles.

Large purple/green bag in chunky cotton chenille øø 30 × 18 cm (12 × 7″) approx, using 5 mm (US 8) needles.

Materials
70–100 g total yarn weight approx, according to yarn and size required.
2 medium size double-pointed needles (see sizes above).

Abbreviations See page 10.

BASIC PATTERN

(All one piece) Cast on 65 sts.
   Purl 1 row.
Row 1 RS (K1, m1, K14, sk2po, K14, m1) twice, K1.
Row 2 Purl.
   Rep these 2 rows throughout, changing cols as

103 Chevron knitted bags (pattern project 9)

shaping diagram

cast off completed hem

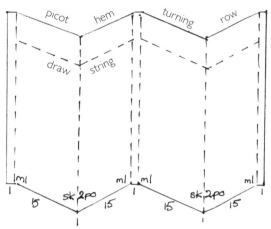

cast on row

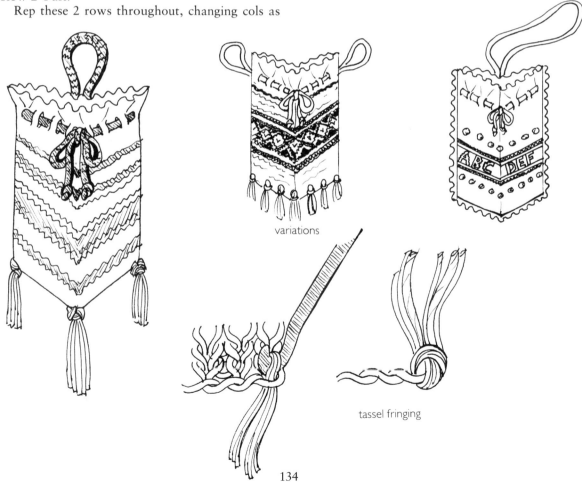

variations

tassel fringing

134

required every few rows, to produce your own col sequence of chevron stripes. Cont until bag is approx 3 cm (1¼") shorter than final length required.

Drawstring row (RS facing)
K1, (yf, K2tog) 7 times, yf, sk2po (yf, K2tog) 7 times, yf. Repeat from * to *, K1.
Next row Purl.
Next 4 rows Work rows 1 and 2 of patt twice.

Picot hem turning row
As drawstring row.
Next row Purl.
Next row RS (K1, skpo, K13, m1, K1, m1, K13, K2tog) twice, K1.
Next row Purl.
Next row Rep last RS row. Cast off.

MAKING UP

Join side seam neatly, darning in all loose ends. Fold picot hem to inside along turning row, and catch down to inside edge of bag.

Make drawstring cord in french knitting as follows:
Using 2 med. size dbl ptd needles, cast on 3 sts, and K1 row.
*Without turning work slide sts to RH end of needle, pull yarn tightly across back of work and K to end of row.
Repeat from * until cord is required length (e.g. 90 cm (35") approx.)
K3tog and pull yarn through loop.
Darn in ends of yarn (if you like, thread a bead onto each end of cord as added decoration).
Thread cord through holes in drawstring row, knot both cord ends and tie into bow, leaving hanging loops at back or sides of bag.
Decorate bag with tassels or fringing as required, using 3 strands of yarn for each tassel, as shown.

Variations
Add fair isle or slipstitch patterns, swiss darning, embroidery, raised stitches and relief effects, lacy motifs, fancy edgings, etc.

TURQUOISE VISCOSE RIBBON BAG

This turquoise bag is worked in stripes. Use it as an example to help you build up confidence before tackling your own design variations. The final

measurement is approximately 26 × 15 cm and the tension (optional) is 17 stitches and 25 rows to 10 cm.

Materials
60 g col A turq chunky viscose ribbon yarn ★★
60 g col B turq/lilac/gold metallic ribbon yarn ★★ ⊗
Small amount of other colours:
C fern green chunky cotton chenille ∅∅
D lilac chunky viscose ribbon yarn ★★
E purple chunky viscose ribbon yarn ★★
1 pair size 6 mm (US 10) needles and 2 medium size double-pointed needles.

To work
Using size 6 mm needles and A, cast on 65 sts and P1 row.
Commence with basic chevron bag patt as set in patt rows 1 and 2.
Work stripes as foll:
Rows 1–6 col A.
Row 7 RS, col B: Work sl st patt, i.e. *K1B, m1B, (K1B, s1P) 7 times, s1K, K2togB, psso, (s1P, K1B) 7 times, m1B, rep from * to last st, K1B. Cont in basic chevron patt as before, work 3 rows B, 2A, 1C, 1D, 2E, 1D, 1C, 3A, 2B, 1A.
Next row RS, cols A + C, i.e. *K1A, m1A, (K1C, K1A) 7 times, s1K, K2togC, psso, (K1A, K1C) 7 times, m1A, rep from * to last st, K1A. Cont in basic patt, work 1 row A, 1E, 2D, 1E, 2A, 2B.
Next row RS, col A: Work sl st patt as in row 7, using A instead of B.
Work 3 rows A.
Still using A, complete as for basic patt, beg with drawstring row.

CHEVRON SHAPED BAG WITH PICOT EDGING

Measurements
Small—22 × 16 cm (8½ × 6").
Med—26 × 18 cm (10 × 7").
Large—30 × 20 cm (12 × 8").

Materials
70 (85, 100) g thick silk/wool (see page 155), or aran weight yarn ④ (knitting kits also available—see page 155.)
1 pair 5 mm needles and set of 4 dble ptd needles size 5 mm (US 8).

Tension

18 sts and 26 rows to 10 cm (4″) over st st, using 5 mm (US 8) needles. As tension is not critical for this pattern, work to your normal tension.

Abbreviations See page 10.

mb—make large bobble as follows: (K1, P1) 4 times in next st. Pass 1st, 2nd, 3rd, 4th, 5th, 6th & 7th sts *in this order* over 8th st.

For small bobble: (K1, P1) twice into next st. Pass 1st, 2nd & 3rd sts *in this order* over 4th st.

FRONT BAG

With size 5 mm (US 8) needles, cast on 33 (37, 41) sts. P1 row.

Row 1 (RS) K1, m1, K14 (16, 18), sk2po, K14 (16, 18) m1, K1.

Row 2 & every WS row P, unless otherwise stated. Rep these 2 rows 3 times (8 rows).

Row 9 (ridge pattern) P1, m1, P14 (16, 18) s1P, P2tog, psso, P14 (16, 18) m1, P1.

Row 10 Knit.

Row 11 As row 1.

Row 13 (small bobbles) K1, m1, K2 (4, 6), (mb, K3) 3 times, sk2po & mb in same st, (K3, mb) 3 times, K2 (4, 6) m1, K1.

Row 15 As row 9.

Row 16 Knit.

Rows 17 & 19 As row 1.

Row 21 (large bobble diamond pattern) K1, m1, K10 (12, 14), (mb, K1) twice, sk2po & mb in same st, (K1, mb) twice, K10 (12, 14), ml, K1.

Row 23 K1, m1, K11 (13, 15), mb, K2, sk2po & mb in same st, K2, mb, K11 (13, 15), m1, K1.

Row 25 K1, m1, K12 (14, 16), mb, K1, sk2po & mb in same st, K1, mb, K12 (14, 16), m1, K1.

Row 27 K1, m1, K14 (16, 18), sk2po & mb in same st, K14 (16, 18), m1, K1.

Row 29 (small diamond eyelet pattern) K1, m1, K6 (8, 10), yf, K2tog, K6, sk2po, K6, K2tog, yf, K6 (8, 10), ml, K1.

Row 31 K1, m1, K6 (8, 10), (yf, K2tog) twice, K4, sk2po, K4, (K2tog, yf) twice, K6 (8, 10), m1, K1.

Row 33 K1, m1, K8 (10, 12), yf, K2tog, K4, sk2po, K4, K2tog, yf, K8 (10, 12), m1, K1.

Rows 35 & 37 As row 1.

Work 0 (6, 12) more rows, keeping to patt as set in row 1.

Work *top edge* of bag as follows, cont to P all WS rows:

Row 1 (drawstring eyelets) K1, (yf, K2tog) 7 (8, 9) times, yf, sk2po, (yf, K2tog) 7 (8, 9) times, yf, K1.

Rows 3 & 5 As row 1 of patt.

Row 7 (Picot hem turning row)—as drawstring row.

Row 9 K1, skpo, K13 (15, 17), m1, K1, m1, K13 (15, 17), K2tog, K1.

Row 11 Cast off.

BACK BAG

Work as front until end of row 20.

Row 21 (diamond eyelets) K1, m1, K8 (10, 12), yf, K2tog, K4, sk2po, K4, K2tog, yf, K8 (10, 12), m1, K1.

Row 23 K1, ml, K8 (10, 12). (yf, K2tog) twice, K2, sk2po, K2, (K2tog, yf) twice, K8 (10, 12), m1, K1.

Row 25 K1, m1, K10 (12, 14), yf, K2tog, K2, sk2po, K2, K2tog, yf, K10 (12, 14), m1, K1.

Row 27 As row 1 of patt.

Cont as for front from row 29 onwards.

TO MAKE UP

Join side edges between top and drawstring level.

Make picot hem by folding top edge to inside along upper row of eyelet holes, and catch down hem around inside edge.

Row 1 (picot edge) With RS of bag facing, using dble ptd 5 mm needles, pick up and K80 (92, 104) sts around side edges and lower edge, picking up sts from F and B tog, thus joining side seams at the same time.

Row 2 Purl.

Row 3 Knit, adding a m1 inc at each corner and either side of central chevron point so that edging lies flat.

Row 4 Purl.

Row 5 Make picot edge *turning row*: K1 (yf, K2tog), rep to last st, yf, K1.

Row 6 Purl, working a dec at both corners, and s1P, p2tog, psso at chevron point.

Row 7 Knit.

Row 8 Cast off Kwise and catch down to RS as neatly as possible.

Make french knitted cord (see page 52) and thread through drawstring eyelets, knotting ends to stop cord pulling through.

Tie bow at CF and pull up drawstring to required length.

Rag knitted jacket.

Short-sleeved summer tops in wave stitch: (left) original version by the author; (right) variation in longer length with side slits knitted by Carole Fisher. Both designs are knitted in cotton ribbon yarns, space dyed by the author and Carole Fisher.

Multi-textured jacket (Photo: Raymond Palmer).

Drop-shoulder all-in-one jacket with cable detail.

Sleeveless jacket with padded picot edging. Short and longer length versions in three colourways.

*Multi-colour chevron and slip stitch coat with
bell motifs* (Photo: Raymond Palmer).

Pattern Project 10 ✕ ✕ ✕

All-in-one chevron-shaped sweater with long sleeves

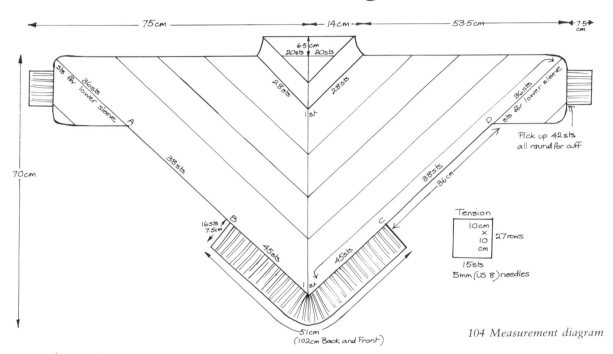

104 Measurement diagram

See colour section

Measurements
One size to fit up to 102 cm/40″ bust.
Finished length from CB. Neck to lower edge 70 cm/27½″.
Sleeve length from CB neck 75 cm/29½″.

Materials
550–600 g approx total weight in mixed DK & chunky yarns or doubled finer yarns, using 150 g approx of main col for neckline, cuffs and lower welt. Perfect for using up oddments. Use sweater variations shown in colour section as a guide to choosing your own selection of mixed textures and colour tones. Basic pattern shaping only is included here to encourage you to plan your own stitch pattern sequence, or you may prefer to work in simple stocking stitch throughout. (However, complete knitting kits with precise row by row

patterns for this style are available by mail order from 20th Century Yarns in selected colourways and mixed yarn textures.) (See page 155.)
    2 circular needles size 5 mm (US 8).
    Set of 4 needles size 4 mm (US 6) & 5 mm (US 8).
    4 stitch holders.

Tension
15 sts and 27 rows to 10 cm (4″) approx over asstd yarns and stitch patterns using size 5 mm (US 8) needles.
Abbreviations See page 10.

MAIN BODY

Starting at B neck and working *back & forth* on size 5 mm (US 8) circular needle, cast on 1 st.
Row 1 Inc in F & B of st (3 sts).

137

Row 2 and every foll WS row Purl, unless otherwise instructed.
Row 3 K1, m1, K1, m1, K1 (5 sts).
Row 5 K1, m1, K1, m1, mark next st and K (CB axis), m1, K1, m1, K1 (9 sts).
Row 7 K1, m1, K to marker, m1, K1 (axis st) m1, K to last st, m1, K1 (13 sts).
Cont to inc on RS rows (as row 7), changing yarn, col and st patt every few rows as required until there are 57 sts on needle, keeping axis st in st st throughout.
Row 30 Cast on 56 sts at beg of WS row, and P across all sts (113 sts).
Row 31 K1, m1, K27 to marker, m1, K CB axis st, m1, K27, m1, mark next st and K (shoulder axis), m1, K27, m1, mark next st and K (CF axis) m1, K to last st, m1, K1 (121 sts).
Row 32 Purl.
Row 33 K1, m1, work to 1st marker, m1, K1 (axis st) m1, work to 2nd marker, m1, K1 (axis st), m1, work to 3rd marker, m1, K1 (axis st), m1, K to last st, m1, K1 (129 sts). Cont to inc on RS rows (as row 33), changing yarns etc as required until there are 481 sts on needle. (Split sts between 2 circular needles, as st Nos increase). End with WS row, dec 1 st at both ends of row (479 sts).
Next row (RS) Slip 36 sts onto 1st stitch holder. *Rejoin yarn. Cast off 167 sts, marking 39th and 129th sts with contrast thread. Break off yarn. Slip next 36 sts onto stitch holder*. Cast off shoulder axis st and slip next 36 sts onto 3rd stitch holder. Rep from * to *.

MAKING UP

Join L shoulder seam invisibly from RS with mattress st (page 152) half st in from edges to resemble axis sts on opposite shoulder, matching patts and cols neatly. Fold sweater along shoulder axis and join underarm seams between stitch markers and contrast thread markers (AB & CD on fig. 97c).

Lower sleeves

Using set of 4 size 5 mm (US 8) needles, transfer stitches for R sleeve from stitch holder onto needles (72 sts). Work inverted underarm chevrons as follows, *starting and finishing row at shoulder axis, and working back and forth, not in rounds, gradually dec sts.* (See fig. 97d.)
Row 1 (RS) K1, skpo, K30 (to within 3 sts of underarm), skpo, K2tog and mark this st (forming new underarm axis st), K2tog, K to last 3 sts, K2tog, K1 (67 sts). Turn.
Row 2 (WS) Purl. Turn.
Row 3 K1, skpo, work to within 2 sts of axis st, K2tog, K axis st, skpo, work to last 3 sts, K2tog, K1 (63 sts). Turn.
Row 4 Purl or patt, keeping axis st in st st. Turn.
Cont to dec on RS rows (as row 3), changing yarns, cols & st patt as before, until 11 sts rem.
Next RS row K1, skpo, K2tog, K axis st, skpo, K2tog, K1.
Next row (WS) As row 4.
Next row K1, (K2tog, K1) twice. Cast off.
Rep for L sleeve.

Cuffs

With set of 4 size 4 mm (US 6) needles and main col, pick up 42 sts around lower sleeve opening and work in K3, P3 rib for 7½ cm (3"). Cast off loosely in rib.

Lower edge welt

With 2 size 4 mm (US 6) needles and main col, cast on 16 sts and work in sideways rib as follows:
Rows 1 & 2 Knit.
Row 3 Purl.
Rows 4 & 5 Knit.
Row 6 Purl.
Rep rows 1–6 until ribbing measures 102 cm (40") (unstretched). Sew or graft first and last rows tog to form a circle. Knit or sew welt edges to lower edge of sweater, picking up 1 st from cast off edge for every 2 rows of rib. At CF and CB ease 6 rows into *each* of centre 3 sts at both axis points so that outer welt edges lie flat.

Neckline

With set of 4 size 4 mm (US 6) needles and main col, rejoin yarn to L shoulder with RS facing and pick up and knit 28 sts from L front neckline, 1 st at CF axis (mark this st), 28 sts from R front neckline, 20 sts from R back neckline, 1 st at CB axis (mark) and 20 sts from L back neckline (98 sts).
Round 1 Knit.
Round 2 K to 2 sts before CF axis st, skpo, K axis st, K2tog, K to end of round. Rep rounds 1 & 2 for 4 cm (1½") (12 rounds approx). Then work straight for 5 cm (2") (16 rounds approx). Finally work m1 incs instead of decs on every alt round at axis sts for 4 cm (1½"). Cast off loosely. Fold neckline in half to WS and hem down.

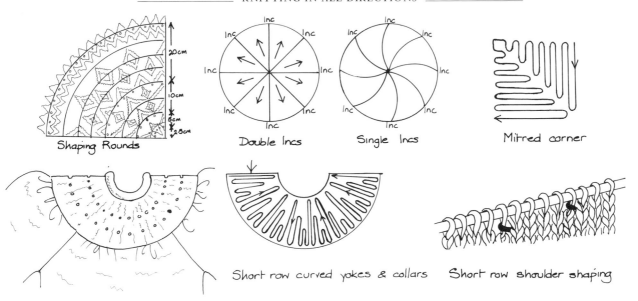

105 Circles and short rows

CIRCLES

Circles can be worked either from the middle if you increase at regular intervals outwards or start from the outside circumference, decreasing at regular intervals inwards. Naturally it makes sense to use a circular needle or set of four double-pointed needles so that the circle can be worked in rounds without any seams. Double shapings are always worked unless you want a decorative swirl pattern. This is formed by single shapings. Fine lacy knitted mats and doilies often incorporate swirl patterns, and are fascinating to study closely to see exactly how the decorative pattern helps to form the circular shape (see Marianne Kinzel's *First and Second Book of Modern Lace Knitting* for intricate circular patterns).

Alternatively, try making circles with shaping 'rounds' at ever doubling intervals from the centre outwards, for example, starting with nine stitches, double to 18 stitches, work 2.5 cm (1″) and double to 36 stitches. Work 5 cm (2″) and double to 72 sts, work 10 cm (4″) and double to 144 sts, and so on. Elizabeth Zimmerman's beautifully simple 'Pi' shawl using this principle is included in two of her wonderfully witty knitting books: *The Knitters Workshop* and *The Knitters Almanac*, which outline her innovative approach to shaping and technique. Don't miss them!

LONG AND SHORT ROWS

Short rows are knitted only partway before you turn and knit back along the row, still keeping all unworked stitches on the needles. This process can be repeated as often as required, knitting progressively fewer or greater numbers of stitches until the whole row is brought back into action again. It is often used to produce darts and wedge shaped sections of knitting which can be combined in various ways for shaping purposes. Starting with flat shaping applications, try making smoothly sloped, rather than stepped shoulder seams (see pattern instructions on page 69, 70) or use for row adjustments and mitred corners. You can also knit *curved* shapes such as yokes and collars by combining consecutive wedges of short row knitting—or even complete circles, if you don't mind the seam.

The turning position on short rows will cause a small lacy hole unless you prefer to disguise it by wrapping the yarn around the next stitch as follows: Work to turning position, yf, sl next st Pwise, yb, ret sl st to LH needle, turn.
On first long row pick up wrap showing on RS of work and Ktog with st above.

In the next chapter you will see how short rows can also be used for three-dimensional shaping.

139

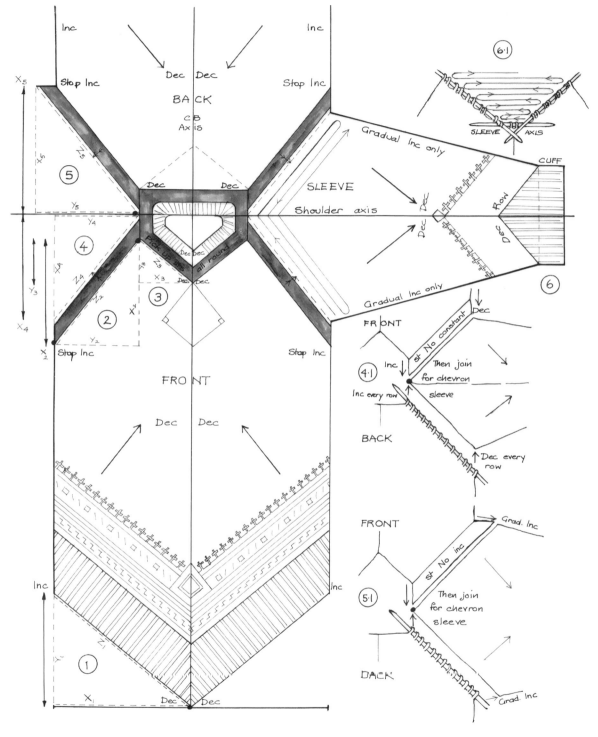

106 Raglan-sleeved chevron project

Pattern Project 11 ✗ ✗ ✗ ✗

Raglan-sleeved chevron project

Figure 106 and colour plate 10 show an example of this chevron project using the following construction and working method. It demands a fair amount of mathematical competence in the planning stages but can be adapted to any size or length you require.

Measurements for tunic length chevron sweater (colour plate 10)

To fit sizes 86–97 cm/34–38″ bust.
91–102 cm/36–40″ hips.
Finished chest measurement 112 cm/45½″.
Finished length from CB neck to point 100 cm/39½″.
(Shorten to conventional sweater length if you prefer.)
Sleeve length from CB neck to wrist 76 cm/30″.

Materials

Main colour —indian red   375 g   DK Cotton
       —plum   125 g   Chenille øø
       —mole   50 g   (See stockists)
       —black   25 g
       —clover   oddments DK
       —grey/purple   weight cotton ③
1 pair each size $3\frac{1}{4}$ mm (US 3) and $2\frac{3}{4}$ mm (US 2) needles or circular needles.
Set of 4 double-pointed needles size $2\frac{3}{4}$ mm.
(See relevant colour chart fig. 62. See also fig. 101 and colour plate 11 for a sleeveless variation in DK cotton).

Working

Basic pattern guidelines only given here—for experienced knitters to work out stitch and row calculations for themselves. The concept is based on using Pythagoras' Theorem (formula $x^2 + y^2 = z^2$, see diagram)—that is, the square root of $(x^2 + y^2) = z$, which provides the measurement of the diagonal from which to calculate the number of sts required. Mathematically inclined knitters will find this easier, but the triangles to work from are marked on the diagram and it becomes a simple matter of applying the formula.

Tension swatch and diagram to scale of measurements are essential to predict the final garment shape, since stitch to row tension ratios, related to the frequency of chevron decreases will produce right angled triangles with varying angles. Try also re-calculating decreases and increases to obtain a right angle at the lower point (i.e. isosceles triangles 45°/45°/90°).

Diagram construction and working method

1 To obtain the correct number of stitches the measurement of y_1 has to be worked out:

$$\frac{\text{Half F/B width} \times \text{row tension for 1 cm}}{\text{rows for dec of 1 st in this section} \times \text{stitch tension for 1 cm}}$$

e.g. tension 20 sts and 32 rows to 10 cm, basic chevron dec of 1 st per 2 rows per section, F/B width 56 cm. Divide by 10 for st and row tension to 1 cm = 2 sts and 3.2 rows. Continue calculation:

$$y_1 = \frac{28 \times 3.2}{2 \times 2} = \frac{89.6}{4} = 22.4$$

$$x^2 = 28 \text{ cm} \times 28 \text{ cm} = 784$$

$$y^2 = 22.4 \text{ cm} \times 22.4 \text{ cm} = 501.76$$

$$z^2 = 784 \times 501.76 = 1285.76$$

$$\therefore z_1 = \sqrt{1285.76}$$

$$z_1 = 35.85 \text{ cm} \times 2 \text{ (st tension for 1 cm)}$$
$$= 71.7 \text{ sts per section.}$$

$$\text{Ratio: } \frac{x_1}{y_1} = \frac{28}{22.4} = 1.25 \ (= \frac{x_2}{y_2} = \frac{x_3}{y_3} \ldots)$$

NOTE: The lower angle is reflected in the shape of the V-neck—but the shallower the lower angle, the steeper the armhole. The width of the neck determines the length of the raglan armhole (or vice

versa), related to the F/B width. Therefore it determines also the width of the sleeves at underarm level. (Variations of sleeve width see 4.1 and 5.1)

For the construction of the diagram the neck width (neck measurement + band and border) should be established first, then the raglan armhole can be worked out, angles applying as for lower edge.

2 $x_2 = \dfrac{x_1}{y_1} \times (x_1 - x_3)$

$z_2 \times$ st tension for 1 cm = No. of sts to be picked up along armhole for sleeve per section.

3 $y_3 = \dfrac{y_1}{x_1} \times x_3$

$z_3 \times$ st tension for 1 cm = No. of sts for neck per section

4 Narrower sleeve
z_4 = same as for 2, No of sts for sleeve per section.
4.1 Inc 1 st every row at neck edge for required measurement to shoulder axis and dec 1 st every row at side edge.

5 Wider sleeve
(x_5 = measurement armhole to shoulder axis)
$y_5 = \dfrac{y_1}{x_1} \times x_5$

$z_5 \times$ st tension for 1 cm = No of sts for sleeve per section (= sts picked up + inc).
5.1 Inc 1 st every row at neck edge (as 4.1) and start gradual inc at side edge to obtain No. of sts required for z_5.

6 Cuff shaping
Work dec row to No. of sts required for measurement straight across at cuff level.
6.1 Starting at axis, using short row technique in reverse, bring in 2 sts more at end of each row.

Pattern Project 12

Fitted sweater with bell-patterned yoke

(Back cover illustration)
A challenging design project suitable for advanced knitters only. Read Chapters 18 & 19 first for explanation of shaping techniques used.

Measurements
To fit bust 86–91 cm/34–36".
To fit waist 69–74 cm/27–29".
Finished length from CB neck 53 cm/21".

Materials
Mixed yarns: mainly wool/silk ⑤ chunky weight or doubled finer weight yarns and chunky cotton chenille ⊘⊘⊘.
Total weight approx 700 g.
1 pair each size 4 mm (US 6) and 5 mm (US 8) needles, long circular needle size 5 mm and set of 4 dbl ptd needles size 4 mm.

Tension
Average of 17 sts and 24 rows to 10 cm (4") over st st, using assorted yarns and size 5 mm (US 8) needles.

Sleeves
1 Using 4 mm (US 6) needles and cotton chenille, cast on 1 st. Working in K1, P1 rib, inc to 14 sts over 2 cm ($\frac{3}{4}$") approx. Cast on 13 sts, then work straight for 6 cm ($2\frac{1}{4}$") (reverse position of point on 2nd sleeve by working 1 more row before casting on extra sts). Change to 5 mm (US 8) needles and inc in every st across row.
2 Plan side edge shaping on knitters graph paper or full size paper patt, drawing in required curve, then breaking it down into sts and rows. Work to position of st division at shoulder, using chosen yarns and st patts.

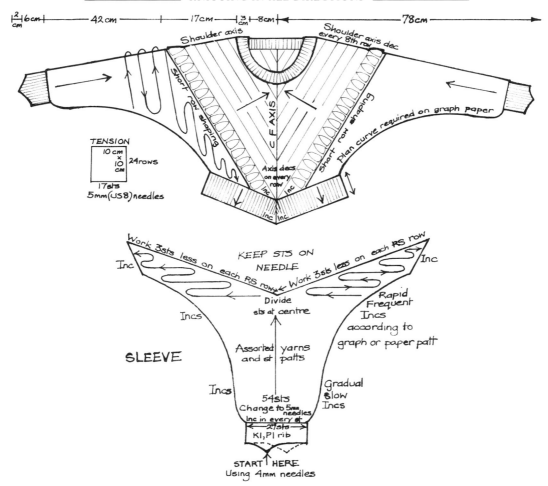

107 *Fitted sweater with bell-patterned yoke—rough outline to working method*

3 Working short row shaping at top edge as shown on sleeve diagram, and inc at side edge as set, complete both halves of sleeve, keeping all sts on needle.

4 Work bell patt (see page 65) also inc at both ends of row. Hold sts. Work 2nd paired sleeve.

Yoke

Using circular needle, transfer sts from both sleeves and beg yoke. Mark CF, CB and L & R shoulder axis. Work sk2po dec on *every* round at CF & CB to form steeply angled chevron shaping, and also at halfway shoulder point on every 8th round approx for shallow shaping.

Neck

Plan neck shaping on graph paper, or work to paper patt. Work back and front neck shaping separately.

MAKING UP

Join underarm seams.

Neckband

Using set of 4 dble ptd 4 mm needles, pick up even No. of sts all round neck and work in K1, P1 rib for 3 cm (1¼"). Cast off loosely in rib.

Lower welt

Using set of 4 dble ptd 4 mm needles, pick up even No. of sts all round lower edge and work in K1, P1 rib for 6.5 cm (2½"), inc each side of CF & CB sts to form symmetrical chevron shaping. Cast off loosely in rib.

143

yf (lacy holes)
or m1 (invisible) incs

Inc Inc

Dec Dec

K2 tog

ssk or skpo

108 Using flares and godets

20
Draped and gathered effects

Now we're going to think about integral methods of shaping within the row to give extra fullness. In dressmaking it would be impossible to achieve this effect without incorporating separate pieces of fabric into the garment. The nearest equivalent would be obtained by draping fabric on the bias grain, but in knitting one continuous length of yarn can be used to produce complex, three-dimensional shapes. Complete fitted garments can be made without the use of a single seam if you so wish.

109 Textured jacket with flared peplum designed and knitted by Maureen O'Dwyer

*110 Sleeveless jacket with peplum. (*Photo by Raymond Palmer*)*

KNITTED FLARES AND GODETS

These are used for fluted shaping on items such as skirts, sleeves, coats and jacket peplums (see colour section and fig. 109). They can either be constructed sideways using short rows as explained in the previous chapter, or worked upwards, or downwards, increasing or decreasing as required. It is simplest to work downwards, for example, when increasing from a fitted waist, the shaping of each flare or godet can be worked until the required length and width is reached by eye, whereas when working upwards stitch numbers have to be

carefully calculated in advance in order to fit correctly. Because of this it can be preferable to work the fitted body section of the garment upwards first, starting at the waist with a temporary cast on method (see page 28). Then, after completing this section, pick up stitches along the temporary cast on row and start working downwards in the opposite direction. The join will be completely invisible and enables you to keep your options open until the last minute.

You can also choose whether to use invisible increases (m1) or lacy increases (yf), or pick out

146

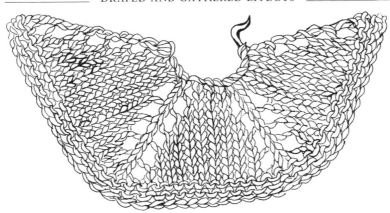

111 Knitted flares

shaping lines even more strongly with narrow purl borders between increases. Alternatively, pinpoint godets with contrasting yarn textures or colours.

When making flares, the more the increases can be spread among the stitches in the row, the better the garment will hang. Take pot luck and guess the degree of flare, or calculate accurately as follows: If hem width is to be three times the original fitted measurement—for example, at waist—measure the distance required from waist to hem and convert into rows using your tension swatch. Calculate the number of extra stitches needed at hem. Decide how many pairs of increases to make in each increase row, (single increases for spiral flares), and divide into the number of extra stitches needed altogether to find the number of increase rows. Divide this number into the number of rows from waist to hem to find how often increases should be worked, e.g.,

Tension = 20 sts/28 rows per 10 cm (using DK yarn)

Total waist inc. ease	= 75 cm
	$= 75 \times \dfrac{20}{10}$ sts
	= 150 sts
Triple width hem	$= 150 \times 3 = 450$ sts
No. of extra sts	= 450 − 150
	= 300 sts
No. of incs in each inc row	= say 12,
	i.e. 6 groups of 2
$\dfrac{300}{12}$	= 25 inc rows

Distance required from waist to hem = 72 cm

No. of rows from waist to hem $= 72 \times \dfrac{28}{10} =$ 201.6 (say 202 rows)

Therefore, frequency of inc rows $= \dfrac{202}{25} = 8$ r2

There will be 12 incs in every 8th row with the first 2 rows worked plain.

Try working a small sample to get the hang of things first.

Cast on 13 sts. Work 2 rows straight in st st.

Row 3 Inc row K1, (yf, K3, yf, K1) 3 times. Purl every alt row.

Row 5 K1, (yf, K5, yf, K1) 3 times.

Row 7 K1, (yf, K7, yf, K1) 3 times.

Continue to increase in this manner.

Change colour every few rows if you like, or try a few ml increases to see which you prefer.

Finish with 2 rows of garter stitch to stop the edge rolling, then cast off.

GATHERS, FRILLS AND FLOUNCES

Gathers produce sudden changes in width within given edges. These are simple to achieve by working single increases or decreases regularly across the row as required. Horizontal gathers are used to give fullness above a fitted cuff or waistband welt; at the top of a sleevehead; or below a shoulder yoke. Often they are combined with a change of stitch and needle size. Sometimes these last two factors are sufficient on their own to produce gathers, without any stitch increases being necessary. Gathers generally offer a much easier way of controlling fullness and coping with calculations than fitted shapes, since only basic rectangular shaped pieces are necessary. For example, a wide straight sleeve can be gathered instantly into a fitted cuff requiring half or even a quarter of the original stitch number by working K2tog in every stitch across the next 1 (or 2) rows. (See multi-colour coat sleeve on colour section). Continue in rib for desired length on needles two sizes smaller. Gathered sleeveheads solve the problem of fitted sleevecap calculations and can easily be adjusted to fit perfectly. Concentrate the gathers around the top half of the armhole, but never gather around the underarm area—it looks amateurish and is uncomfortable. Gathers can also be worked at cuffs, necklines and waistlines to produce decorative edgings such as frills, collars, ruffs and peplums.

Ruffled edgings are sideways knitted vertical gathers attached to a straight edge at one side. The ruffled effect is accentuated by using short rows and a reverse stocking stitch welt pattern (see page 113 for detailed instructions).

Ruching consists of narrow bands of heavy gathers interspersed by straight knitting, and is often worked as an allover pattern. It gives a pronounced three-dimensional effect (see page 49 for instructions).

If you haven't already started jotting down a few ideas which appeal to you, do it now. Rough out a few shapes, then think how you can individualize them to suit yourself with the help of this chapter.

Section 4
FINISHING AND MAKING UP

21

Old and new techniques to achieve that professional finish

If I had to choose between an innovative sweater with a poor finish, and one that was dull but beautifully finished, I'd go for design originality every time. If the design doesn't attract, you probably won't bother to look closely enough to notice the finish anyway. But how much more rewarding to see a good design where the finish bears close inspection too—and why not, when it takes comparatively little extra time and effort to achieve? Unfortunately, many knitters tend to rush the finishing stages in their eagerness to see how the completed item will look. Don't be impatient. When you've lavished so much care and attention on the knitting, you owe it to yourself to take care with the final stages too. I find the following tips contribute most effectively to a good all round finish. Many others can be found in any stitch dictionary or book on knitting technique, but these are my personal favourites.

BLOCKING

Blocking is a process of dampening and shaping knitting to set it into the required shape. You won't believe the difference it makes to the finish until you've tried it yourself! Steaming or pressing methods are well known, but I find cold blocking gives the best results and is kinder to the yarn.

Cold blocking method—no iron needed

1 Cover any large flat pinnable surface with a clean cloth and layers of padding if necessary. A table, bed or carpet will do, or try packing cartons, cork boards or polystyrene sheets. Blocking boards with a square grid are available to make accurate pinning out easier.

2 Pin out corners of each knitted piece, right side up, to required length and width measurement. Use a tape measure or marked squares to guide you, and long glass-headed pins. Place pins sloping outwards to anchor knitting firmly, gradually adding more pins around edges, and stretching or easing knitting into required shape until pins are roughly 2 cm (1″) apart. Avoid any ribbed areas where elasticity must be retained.

3 When satisfied, spray with a fine-misted water spray until knitting is thoroughly damp.

4 Leave until bone dry—1 to 2 days—then remove pins carefully.

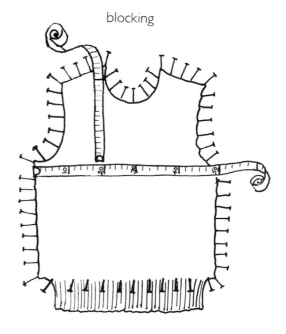

blocking

Some items can be stretched without pins, using a mould instead, for example, berets with a plate inside, pull-on hats over a pudding basin. Other moulds can be used for small items, such as, small pebbles or cotton wool balls for embossed leaf patterns. Use your initiative!

MAKING UP

Ladder or mattress stitch seam
No one can pretend that sewing up seams is exciting, but there is a definite satisfaction in stitching a seam which promptly becomes invisible from the right side—and it's so easy to do! With the right sides facing you, pick up horizontal bars alternately on both pieces to be joined as shown, working either half a stitch or one stitch in from the edge, and pulling the yarn through loosely to make horizontal rungs between the pieces. Pull the yarn up firmly every few stitches, then stretch slightly to add 'give' to the seam. Once tried, you'll never want to go back to other seam methods—even complicated patterns are easy to match when you can see what you're doing so clearly.

Back stitch seams
Widely used but often bulky, back stitch seams are ideal when you require strength and ridigity, for example, firm shoulder seams to support sleeves that are not meant to stretch.

Knitted and raised seams
Occasionally you may want to make a feature of a seam rather than hide it. This can be done in several ways, and is particularly effective on shoulder seams. With wrong sides together, pick up a cast off stitch from front and back shoulder edges, and knit these two stitches together. Continue along the cast off edges picking up, knitting and then casting off as you go. The resulting seam will be stretchy and neat, and can also be worked with right sides together if you prefer the seam edges to be hidden inside. Alternatively, do not cast off the shoulder seams before knitting them together. Hold both sets of stitches together on the needles with the points facing the same way (WS or RS together as preferred). Knit together one stitch from front and back needle before proceeding as before.

Shaped shoulder seams (see pages 69 and 139)
These are always superior to conventional stepped

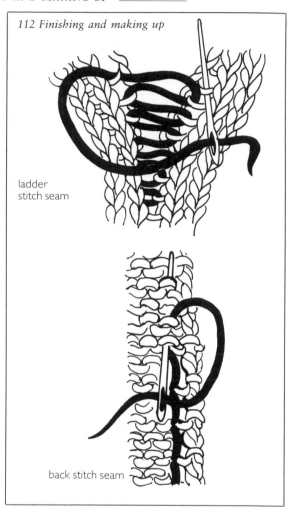

112 Finishing and making up

ladder stitch seam

back stitch seam

shoulder seams and can be used in conjunction with fake or true grafting, or knitted seams.

Hem finishing and edgings (see Chapter 17)

Knit grafting
Grafting is the ideal way to join two pieces of knitting together invisibly, *without making a seam*. The edges are not cast off and a blunt sewing needle is used to link together both sets of stitches with an imitation row which looks exactly like knitting. Practise first with two stocking stitch samples (approximately 20 stitches) knitted in thick plain yarn. As it is easier to understand grafting when the stitches are off the needles, steam or press the samples to discourage unravelling, or fix stitches by

knit grafting

temporarily back stitching across the last-but-one row of knitting.

Thread needle with yarn about four times width of rows.

Work flat, right sides up, with open rows of loops facing each other.

Working from right to left, insert needle as follows:

1 *Up* through 1st lower loop.
2 *Down* 1st upper loop then *up* 2nd upper loop.
3 *Down* 1st lower loop then *up* 2nd lower loop.

Repeat steps **2** and **3** across the work, always working *up, then down through the same loop* and pulling yarn through to match tension of surrounding knitting. Persevere—the results are well worth

the effort of mastering this technique, and it has so many useful and creative applications—from grafted underarms to complex three-dimensional shapes, without a seam in sight!

Fake grafting

This is a good compromise if you don't feel ready for true grafting just yet. Try using it for straight shoulder seams. It resembles grafting on the right side of the work, but the seam is disguised, not eliminated altogether. Proceed as for knit grafting, but with *cast off rows* facing each other, catching stitches from either edge as shown instead of loops. It is also possible to combine the two methods by grafting a row of free loops to a cast off row; this is yet another intermediate stage to true grafting proficiency.

These techniques are only a small selection of those in current use. I could have included others, but this book is not an encyclopaedia of techniques. There are many such books on the market already. Instead, my aim throughout has been to encourage you to adopt a more questioning approach to knitting so that you are able to make your own

113 Designs using colour, shape and texture: (top) *Edwardian influenced design shape with soft two-colour knitted pleats and decorative bobbles;* (bottom) *plaited french knitting accentuating simple style features*

row of knitted bells

reverse stocking stitch
rolled edge

114 *Designs using colour, shape and texture: (top) simple, straight knitted coat and beret with rolled edges at armholes and neck; (bottom) batwing sweater knitted diagonally with chevrons at front*

decisions, and control your knitting rather than letting it control you. If you've worked your way right through the book to this final page, you should now be equipped to design and knit creatively in your own personal style. As your technical skills improve, so the standard of your work will develop artistically too. Every time you master a new technique and discover novel applications for it, you will be opening up extra creative avenues to explore.

Like you, I am still searching and discovering. A lifetime is not enough to pursue every avenue of thought which springs to mind. It's not a question of running out of ideas, but of finding the time to develop more than a few of them. If you have a career as well as family commitments I am sure you know what I mean.

Knitting can be enjoyed on many different levels. Whether you knit simply for relaxation and pleasure or are searching for a deeper fulfilment, I hope this book has helped you to analyse and understand your knitting, and has opened your eyes to the creative possibilities which knitting offers. Now it is over to you to develop your own ideas with confidence in the future. I wish you every success.

Useful addresses

SPECIALIST YARN SHOPS AND SUPPLIERS—BRITAIN

Most suppliers also deal by mail order except * and stock knitting books. Send large SAE for price lists and details of shade cards etc.

Creativity, 45, New Oxford St, London WC1*. and 15, Downing St, Farnham, Surrey, GU9 7PB.

Colourway, 112A, Westbourne Grove, London, W2 5RU. Tel. (01) 229 1432

Ries Wools, 242–3, High Holborn, London, WC1. Tel. (01) 242 7721

Rowan Yarns, Green Lane Mill, Washpit, Holmfirth, W. Yorks (wholesale only)
(*Natural fibre yarns, incl. DK and chunky cotton chenille in wide range of colours; send for list of retail stockists other than those shown above.*)

Yarncraft, Three Ply House, 57A, Lant St, London, SE1 1QN. Tel. (01) 403 1216/1207
(*Natural fibre yarns.*)

20th Century Yarns Ltd, The Red House, Guilsborough, Northants. NN6 8PU. Tel. (0604) 740348
(*Exclusive designer dyed speciality yarns in natural fibres incl. fine & thick pure silk, silk/wool and tussah silk and knitting kits for patts shown on pages 67, 118, 135, 137.*)

Jamieson & Smith Ltd, 90, North Rd, Lerwick, Shetland Isles ZE1 OPQ. Tel. (0595) 3579
(*Authentic shetland wools, including 1 ply weight.*)

Shepherds Purse and Meadows, 2 John St, Bath.

The Dartington Cider Press Centre, Dartington, Totnes, Devon, TQ9 6JE.

Liberty's Knitting Dept, Liberty, Regent St, London, W1R 6AH. Tel. (01) 734 1234.

Designer Yarns, 367 Sauchiehall St, Glasgow, G2, Scotland.

Bobbins, Wesley Hall, Church St, Whitby, Yorkshire.

Up Country, Towngate, Holmfirth, West Yorkshire.

GENERAL SUPPLIERS—BRITAIN

Fibrecrafts, Style Cottage, Lower Eashing, Godalming, Surrey. GU7 2QD. Tel. (04868) 21853.
(*Mail order, callers by appt. only. Needles, ball winders, swifts, knitters' graph paper and excellent range of imported knitting books and magazines.*)

H. W. Peel & Co. Ltd, Norwester House, Fairway Drive, Greenford, Middx. UB6 8PW. Tel. (01) 578 6861.
(*Manufacturers of 'True Knit' knitters graph paper. Trade & Wholesale only; send for list of retail stockists.*)

French Knitter—available from Falcon-by-Post. Westfield Rd, Horbury, Wakefield, W. Yorks. WF4 6HP.

The Button Box, 44, Bedford St, Covent Garden, London WC2E 9HA. Tel. (01) 240 2716/2841
(*Interesting buttons*)

Spinners, Fakenham Rd, Beerley, Dereham, Norfolk. Tel. (0362) 860194. (*Callers by appointment, except Friday and Saturday*)
(*Hard-to-find knitting accessories*)

Thorn Press, The Old Vicarage, Godney, Wells, Somerset, BA5 1RX. Tel. (0458) 32225. (*Callers by appointment only*)
(*Hard-to-find knitting accessories*)

Peapod to Zebras, 4, The Crescent, Hyde Park Corner, Leeds, LS6 2NW. (*Buttons, beads*)

ORGANIZATIONS

Britain

The Knitting Craft Group, PO Box 6, N. Yorks, YO7 1TA.
(*Creative knitting and crochet resources for teachers/students, children and interested knitters.*)

The Knitting and Crochet Guild, Subscription details from Elizabeth Gillet, Membership Secretary, 5, Roman Mount, Roundhay, Leeds, W. Yorks, LS8 2DP.
(*Quarterly magazine*, Slipknot.)

Edinburgh Knitting and Crochet Guild—Julie Matthews, Secretary, 9 Lennie Cottages, Craigs Road, Edinburgh, EH12 0BB.

USA

The Knitting Guild of America—PO Box 166 Knoxville, Tennessee, 37901.

COURSES (RESIDENTIAL/NON-RESIDENTIAL)

Missenden Weekends & Summer School (*incl. courses run by Maggie Whiting*), Missenden Abbey, Gt Missenden, Bucks, HP16 0BD. Tel. (02406) 6811/4037.

Wensum Lodge, King St, Norwich, Norfolk NR1 1QW. Tel. (0603) 666021.

South Hill Park Arts Centre, Bracknell, RG12 4PA. Tel. (0344) 427272.

Styal Workshop, Quarry Bank Mill, Styal, Cheshire, SK9 1LA. Tel. (0625) 527468.

Surrey Heath Adult Education, France Hill Drive, Camberley, Surrey. Tel. (0276) 20145/6.
(*Maggie Whiting fashion & creative knitting courses*)

Knitting Craft Group—see organizations. (*Teachers courses only*)

YARN SHOPS AND SUPPLIERS—USA

For extra addresses see the back lists of knitting magazines

Fiber Works, 313, East 45th St, New York, 10017.

Soft Spectrum, 216, Grand Avenue, Pacific Grove, California.

Country Linens of Vermont, 140, Church St, Burlington, Vermont.

Straw into Gold, 3006, San Pablo Avenue, Berkeley, California.

Tomato Factory Yarn C., 31, Railroad Place, Hopewell, New Jersey 08525.

The Woolgatherer, 1502, 21st St, N.W. Washington, DC, 20036.

Martha Hall, 46, Main St, Yarmouth, Maine, ME, 04096.

Coulter Studios, East 59th St, Manhattan, New York.

The Needlework Attic, 4706 Bethesda Ave., Bethesda, MD, 20814.

Cotton Clouds, Desert Hills 16, Route 2, Safford, AZ, 85546. (*100% cotton yarns*)

The Yarn Barn, 918 Massachusetts, PO Box 334, Lawrence, Kansas 66044.
(*Supplies and advice for fiberartists*)

Dyed in the Wool, Suite 1800, 252, W.37th Street, New York, 10018.
(*Handpainted yarns and solid colours in wool, 100% cotton, silk, mohair, etc.*)

Westminster Trading, 5, Northern Boulevard, Amherst, NH, 03031.

Schoolhouse Press, 6899, Cary Bluff, Pittsville, W1 54466. (*Books, videos, knitting tools, yarns*)

The Stitching Post, 5712, Patterson Ave., Richmond, VA 23226.
(*Knitters' graph paper, silver knitting needles and books*)

Pattern Works, PO Box 1690, Dept V7, Pough Keepsie, New York, 12601. (*Hard-to-find items*)

Tender Buttons, 143, East 62nd St, New York, 10021. (*Buttons*)

The Hands Work, PO Box 386, Pecos, NM, 87552. (*Handmade buttons*)

SPECIALIST BOOK SUPPLIERS

(*Often able to supply imported or difficult-to-obtain books. All do mail order.*)

Britain
Fibrecrafts—see general suppliers. Stocks many American books and magazines on recommended booklist.
The Textile Bookshop, Tynwald Mills, St John's, Isle of Man. Tel. (0624) 71213.
(*Mail order, callers by appointment only.*)
R. D. Franks Ltd, Kent House, Market Place, Oxford Circus, London, W1N 8EJ. Tel. (01) 636 1244/5/6.
Thorn Press—see general suppliers. All Tessa Lorant books.
Crafts of Quality Books, 49 Gelston Point, Burwell Close, London E1 2NR. Tel. (01) 790 1093.

USA
Schoolhouse Press—see general suppliers and magazines. Many difficult to find and British books stocked from recommended booklist.
Ballantine Books, 201 E. 50th Street, Dept JV, 9-1, New York 10022. Selection of British books.
The Stitching Post—see general suppliers.

Bibliography and recommended book list

Books

Bradley, Sue. *Stitches in time*, Orbis, 1986.

Briggs, Maureen. *Knitting: patterns, stitches and styles*, Chancerel, 1976.

Crafts Council. *Running a workshop. Basic business for craftspeople*. 1985.

The Creators 2. *British masquerade*, Nihon Vogue, 1986. (Japanese paperback available from the Crafts Council, 12 Waterloo Place, London in English translation)

Cone, Ferne Geller. *Knit art*, Van Nostrand Reinhold, 1975.

Ellalouf, Sian. *The knitting architect*, Knitting Fever, New York, 1982.

Erikson, Mary Anne & Cohen, Eve. *Knitting by design*, Bantam Books Inc., 1986.

Fassett, Kaffe. *Glorious knitting*, Century Publishing, 1985.

Fee, Jacqueline. *The sweater workshop*, Interweave Press Inc., 1983.

Foale, Marion. *Marion Foale's classic knitwear*, Pelham, 1985.

Gibson-Roberts, Priscilla A. *Knitting in the old way*, Interweave Press, 1985.

Hofstatter, Kirsten. *Everybody's knitting*, Penguin books, 1987.

Kinzel, Marianne. *First book of modern lace knitting*, 1953. Dover reprint, 1972. *Second book of modern lace knitting*, 1961. Dover reprint, 1972.

Lorant, Tessa. *Knitted quilts & flounces*, The Thorn Press, 1982. *The good yarn guide*, The Thorn Press, 1985.

Messent, Jan. *Have you any wool?* Search Press Ltd, 1986.

Price, Lesley Anne. *Kids' knits*, Dorling Kindersley, 1983.

Righetti, Maggie. *Knitting in plain English*, St Martin's Press, New York, 1986.

Stanley Montse. *Knitting your own designs for a perfect fit*, David & Charles, 1982, 1985 (revised). *The handknitter's handbook*, David & Charles, 1986.

The harmony guide to knitting stitches, Lyric Books, 1983; Vol 2, 1987.

The knit kit, Collins, 1985.

Mary Thomas's knitting book, Hodder & Stoughton, 1958; reprinted 1985.

Mary Thomas's book of knitting patterns, Hodder & Stoughton, 1943. Reprinted, 1985.

Walker, Barbara G. *Knitting from the top*, Charles Scribners' Sons, 1972. *Charted knitting designs: a third treasury of knitting patterns*, Charles Scribners' Sons, 1972.

Sampler knitting, Charles Scribners' Sons, 1973.

Walker Phillips, Mary. *Creative knitting: a new art form*, Van Nostrand Reinhold, 1971. Reprinted by Dos Tejedoras; UK distributor, Alison Hodge.

Waller, Jane. *A stitch in time*, Duckworth, 1972.

Wild knitting, Mitchell Beazley, 1979. Emblem paperback edition 1980, reprinted 1982 (now out of print).

Zimmermann, Elizabeth. *Knitting without tears*, Charles Scribners' Sons, 1971. *The knitters' almanac*, Charles Scribners' Sons, 1974. Dover reprint 1981. *Knitting workshop*, Schoolhouse Press, 1981.

MAGAZINES

Vogue Knitting (*3 issues per annum*) on sale in shops and from:
(*Britain*) Vogue Pattern Service, New Lane, Havant, Hants, PO9 2ND.
(*USA*) 161 Avenue of the Americas, New York.

USA

Knitters—(*4 issues per annum*) Golden Fleece Publications, 335 North Main Ave., Sioux Falls, SD57102.

Woolgathering—(*2 issues per annum*) Schoolhouse Press, 6899 Cary Bluff, Pittsville, WI 54466 (Elizabeth Zimmermann and Meg Swansen).

(*All excellent for creative knitters. Titles marked * available in Britain from Fibrecrafts—see under general suppliers*)

The following magazines feature a variety of textile crafts but frequently include knitting:

USA

Threads—(*6 issues per annum*) Taunton Press, 63, South Main St, Newtown, CT 06470.

Britain

Fashion and Craft—(*4 issues per annum*) Blenheim Publications, 1 Quebec Avenue, Westerham, Kent, TN16 1BJ.

Workbox—(*2 issues per annum*) 40 Silver Street, Wiveliscombe, Somerset.

BOOKFINDING SERVICES, SECONDHAND, OUT OF PRINT AND ANTIQUARIAN BOOKS

(*All mail order, callers by appointment only, except for* *. *Catalogues often available.*)

Britain
Doreen Gill, 14, Barnfield Road, Petersfield, Hampshire, GU31 4DQ. Tel. (0730) 62274.

Black Cat Books, 1, Granby Road, Edinburgh, EH16 5NH. Tel. (031) 667 6341.
Judith Mansfield, 60A Darnton Road, London, SW12 9NE. Tel. (01) 673 6635.
Alan Wicks, 'Nimrod', Broyle Lane, Ringmer, Lewes, Sussex BN8 5PQ. Tel. (0273) 812359.
***Willow House Books**, The Cottage Bookshop, 5, Hill Street, Chorley, Lancs. (Avril Whittle). Tel. (025) 7269280 (*or call at shop*).

Approximate yarn requirements

Use quantities shown here as a rough estimate for designs worked in st st. Requirements differ according to yarn and stitches chosen, but silks usually go further than the same weight in wool, whereas mohair, tweed and cotton generally give a lower yield.

DK weight

	81 cm 32″	86 cm 34″	91 cm 36″	97 cm 38″	102 cm 40″
Sleeveless top	250 g	300 g	300 g	350 g	350 g
Round neck sweater	400 g	450 g	500 g	550 g	600 g
Polo neck sweater	+ 50 g per size				
V neck sweater	− 50 g per size				
Cardigan	+ 50 g per size				

4 ply weight

	81 cm 32″	86 cm 34″	91 cm 36″	97 cm 38″	102 cm 40″
Sleeveless top	200 g	250 g	250 g	250 g	300 g
Round neck sweater	300 g	300 g	350 g	350 g	400 g
Polo neck sweater	+ 50 g per size				
V neck sweater	250 g	300 g	300 g	350 g	350 g
Cardigan	350 g	400 g	450 g	450 g	500 g

Aran weight

	81 cm 32″	86 cm 34″	91 cm 36″	97 cm 38″	102 cm 40″
Long sleeved sweater	600 g	700 g	750 g	800 g	850 g

Index